LESSONS IN CLASSICAL DANCE

.

LESSONS IN CLASSICAL DANCE

Sophia Golovkina

Translated by Nigel Timothy Coey

Edited by Joan Lawson

Photographs by Leonid Zhdanov
Notation of the lessons by Nadezhda Vikhareva

DANCE BOOKS   CECIL COURT   LONDON

First published in 1991 by Dance Books Ltd.
9 Cecil Court, London WC2N 4EZ

© 1991 Sophia Golovkina

A CIP catalogue record for this book is available from
the British Library.

ISBN 1 85273 024 2

Design and production in association with
Book Production Consultants,
47 Norfolk Street, Cambridge

Printed and bound in Great Britain by Biddles Ltd, Surrey

Contents

Foreword

Sophia Golovkina is world famous as a Bolshoi Theatre ballerina and the Director of the Moscow Academic Choreographical School. Sophia is also a masterful teacher of the art of classical dance.

Sophia Golovkina started her ballet career at the same place as her pupils – at the Moscow Choreographical School. Upon graduation she was invited to join the Bolshoi Ballet Company. For 27 years she sparkled on the stage in the leading roles in the ballets *Swan Lake, The Nutcracker, Raymonda, The Sleeping Beauty, Bayadère* and *The Humpbacked Horse*.

Sophia was involved in the creation of the contemporary repertory of the ballet company. She performed major parts in ballets produced by Fyodor Lopukhov, Vasily Vainonen, Leonid Lavrovsky and Rostislav Zakharov. Her dancing exuded confidence, buoyancy and exuberance combined with filigree technique.

Fate brought her into contact with eminent Soviet ballet master Fyodor Lopukhov, who produced the ballet *Bright Stream* to the music of Dmitry Shostakovich. Golovkina was the prima ballerina. Lopukhov provided her with encyclopaedic knowledge of the art of dance. He opened before her the fathomless history of the arts, music and choreography, supported her and directed the bold creative initiative of the young ballerina. Fyodor Lopukhov clearly influenced in a major way the formation of Golovkina as a dance personality.

Leaving the stage, Sophia Golovkina returned to her alma mater. A second life began for her as Director and teacher of classical dance.

Here Golovkina has displayed incredible talent as an organiser. Sophia has an enquiring mind and great insight. She is full of initiative and energy.

Sophia Golovkina has made the Moscow School the pace-setter in choreographical teaching methods. Sophia has personally initiated and worked with her colleagues on new ballet productions. She has displayed a talent as a stage director by taking part in the new production of *Coppélia* in 1977, *Vain Precautions (La fille mal gardée)* in 1979 and a number of divertissements which are a big success at the Bolshoi and the Kremlin Palace of Congresses and are included in national and international competitions.

Sophia is a fine teacher and dance theoretician. Since 1960 she has personally taught in the senior grades, training over 70 ballerinas including such stars as Natalya Bessmertnova, Nina Sorokina, Alla Mikhalchenko, Marina Leonova, Nelly Beredina, Galina Stepanenko, Olga Suvorova and Nadezhda Grachova.

Golovkina has found a harmonious blend of immense personal stage experience and theoretical knowledge. She understands all the nuances of the contemporary theatre and the sophistication of contemporary ballet productions. Her pupils are well-trained in the strict academic traditions and possess excellent technique.

This book contains six lessons by Sophia Golovkina and must surely interest all teachers of choreography. Sophia blends lessons in basic technique with stage artistry and expression. The six lessons cited show clearly the way the senior grades are taught. The teaching enchaînements are logically constructed to encapsulate the whole curriculum.

Any teacher has to be a ballet master and compose enchaînements for classical dance lessons. The success of the class depends upon the quality of these. The Golovkina lessons may serve as a guideline.

In conclusion, I would just like to note that the famous Bolshoi Ballet Company, which I have been leading for over 20 years, draws mainly on the Moscow Academic Choreographical School. The world renown of the Bolshoi should by right be shared with the Moscow School which Sophia Golovkina has headed for three decades.

Yuri Grigorovich

Editor's Introduction

Having been privileged to watch Sophia Golovkina's classes, both in the old building behind the Bolshoi Theatre and later in the beautiful new studios and theatre built specially for the Moscow Academic Choreographical School, I know how exciting and valuable her lessons are to those who love and believe that classical dance, performed by Russians, always holds its audiences captive by its beauty of line, sense of movement and dynamic interpretations of mood, emotion, action and character. Sophia Golovkina's lessons are outstanding in the way that they make students draw and feel lines through the steps and poses, until the studio is filled with dance. She achieves this firstly through the detailed attention she pays to the accurate placing of each movement in the total design of an enchaînement, so that the transition from one step or pose to the next is effortless because time is always given to make the transition of weight, balance and placing. Secondly through her use of ports de bras and heads to give direction and lead the patterns. Her own ports de bras are a lesson to all. Thirdly through her insistence that all 'listen and respond to the music'. As Fokine said: 'Students must go to, through and from the notes.' It is these features which excite me about the six lessons she has notated for all who believe in teaching not only technique, but artistry.

Joan Lawson

Teaching Classical Dance to the Senior Grades

Choreography is the art of presenting important ideas and deep images in the weird and wonderful language of dance. That art has made immense strides in recent years, making greater demands on male and female performers alike. Perfect technique is required of all.

Our Soviet school of choreography, while always remaining loyal to the traditions of classical dance, has responded quickly to modern changes in ballet theatre. This is a strength. We continue to draw on the wealth of teaching experience passed down by famous choreographers of the past. And at the same time we seek new roads to refinement in the methodology of teaching classical dance.

The current generation of dance teachers is equipped with a wide range of theoretical knowledge. Many famous dancers of the past have become teachers, and they naturally have plenty of practical experience to offer their protégés. And yet we often find that neither theoretical wisdom nor practice on the stage can guarantee a budding dance master against the problems involved in initiation. In what sequence should he set the various movements? How many times should the pupils repeat a movement in an exercise? What movements form the best enchaînement? How does one make a whole lesson run smoothly? Such are the dilemmas confronting any new teacher.

We have little idea of how the great dance masters of the past constructed their lessons. History has conveyed to us a mere outline of the teaching methods of Carlo Blasis and one lesson by F. Taglioni which he gave his daughter, the great Marie Taglioni.

The pupils of Agrippina Vaganova preserve in memory her lessons. Yet just one of those lessons was fully annotated. It was published in Vaganova's book *The Fundaments of Classical Dance* (published in the West as *Basic Principles of Classical Ballet*).

The lessons of Asaf Messerer (see *Classes in Classical Ballet*, Iskusstvo Publishers, Moscow, 1967) serve merely as a guideline. They are for ballet performers rather than pupils.

Notes to the lessons of many other eminent teachers (Vyazem, Legat, Tikhomirov and Sobeshchanskaya) have unfortunately never been systemised and published, and thus cannot be used by masters of dance today. The sole teaching aid available has been the book *100 Lessons in Classical Dance* by Vera Kostrovitskaya.

I offer here a book for teachers. It contains exercises for six lessons: three for a first year and three for a second year at choreographic schools. They are for the second half of the academic year.

My many years as a teacher have convinced me that the most productive approach is as follows. Studies should be organised in such a way as to present the main material of the curriculum in the first half of the academic year. Movements should be taught in a pure form at a relaxed pace before proceeding to easy enchaînements. Then in the second half of the year, all possible approaches to the given movements are developed. The more complex enchaînements with other movements are learnt. These are more demanding and lengthy, and the speed of execution is increased.

Each step of the teaching has its specific features and difficulties. In the junior and middle grades, our pupils are taught the fundaments of classical dance, study the basic movements, acquire endurance and learn expression. The senior grades make a brand new step. Their lessons summarise all the knowledge and skills mastered over five years, skills so essential for studying the most complex movements of classical dance in the final professional form.

Apart from refining virtuoso technique, work towards artistic expression and feeling for the music acquires great significance, and the artistic individuality of the pupils is developed. We aim at equipping our graduates to start out on an independent artistic road.

The curriculum for the last three grades is full of the most difficult elements in all areas of study. The exercises in the centre focus on all versions of the grand fouetté, and grand fouetté en tournant, the renversé and complex enchaînements of the tours lents. All forms of spin acquire added difficulty: the number of turns in the major poses increases; combined spins along the diagonal and in a circle are introduced; and the speed of the spin increases.

The allegro section is particularly complicated, including the grand jeté and the grand jeté en tournant, the jeté entrelacé, the saut de basque, the grande cabriole, the grand fouetté en tournant, etc. The way a pose is held is varied and comprises all the most difficult movements in classical dance.

We firmly believe that increased efficiency and results from a lesson result, firstly, from good construction of every section (exercise at the barre, exercise in the centre, allegro, and exercise sur les pointes) and, secondly, from an ability to methodically and correctly perform virtuoso enchaînements.

Depending on the curriculum for a particular grade, each section of a lesson has its targets and a specific order for the movements. That order is not arbitrary, but based on the best traditions. The teacher has to arrange a lesson which accounts for the professional and physical capabilities of his pupils. The teacher has to think out how best to arrange and distribute the physical load on separate groups of muscles and ligaments. He must seek an organic co-ordination of strength and dance movements.

The exercise at the barre should take less time than in the middle grades, no more than 25 minutes. Some budding teachers view the exercise at the barre in the senior grades as preparation of the legs and torso for the complex work in the centre which will be required for work in the theatre. At a choreographic school the exercise at the barre should be first and foremost instructive. The movements must blend in such a way as to consolidate what was taught in the previous grades. Pupils need the opportunity to perform the movements absolutely properly with due control. At the same time new complex barre movements are learnt which later form the basis for the exercise in the centre.

The exercise at the barre contains many testing movements. We consider it proper to recommend that pupils warm up the leg muscles and ligaments before a lesson. This enables them to gain greater benefit.

Like many other dance masters, I have devised a special set of exercises for warming up the legs. The set of exercises is based on battements tendus combined with battements tendus pour le pied and battements jetés performed at a slow pace, first in the 1st and then in the 5th position, facing the barre.

There are different opinions as to what movements should commence a lesson in classical dance.

Some, including Vaganova, adhered to a tradition dating from Blasis which says the exercise at the barre should begin with a plié. Other teachers, such as the famous N. Legat, prefer to start a lesson with a battement tendu.

I start off with some demi-pliés and grands pliés, combining them with diverse ports de bras. This is a protracted combination, 3/4 musical metre. It is essential to set the legs and the whole torso working at the same time. A demi-plié, stretching the Achilles tendon, prepares the foot for further loads, and a grand plié stretches and consolidates the hip muscles.

Usually ports de bras follow on from ronds de jambe à terre. I do not set them in the first exercise since both movements (particularly 3rd port de bras) get all the muscles of the torso working well. I have devised various different combinations of demi-pliés and grands pliés which my pupils know off-by-heart. This enables me to save time on explaining the task. I simply say 'plié with battement tendu' or 'plié and relevé', etc.

Much attention should be paid to thorough and proper battements tendus and battements jetés, as those movements develop strength in the legs and elasticity in the feet, while consolidating the correctness of the 5th position for the legs. I set battements tendus along with battements jetés and usually round off the enchaînement with flic-flacs en tournant.

All the exercises prepare the muscles for ronds de jambe à terre and grands ronds de jambe jetés. I follow up ronds de jambe à terre with ports de bras involving the body in all poses up to 90 degrees. Here, at a calm pace, the correctness of the turn of the hips is checked and consolidated when a leg is raised 90 degrees in all directions with various inclinations of the torso.

The next movement – the battement fondu – is to work on one of the basic elements in classical dance, the plié-relevé. Correct execution of this movement is essential for steadiness in all the poses and positions of adagio, spinning, pointe technique, and jumps. I send the pupils from a battement fondu into a battement frappé, with a fast acceleration. In a battement frappé it is important to achieve absolute extension of the foot and abruptness of execution. In this exercise I often demand abrupt turns of the torso, thereby developing litheness and co-ordination.

When practising ronds de jambe en l'air, there should be good fast training of doubles ronds de jambe. I therefore gradually proceed from a calm pace to a fast pace. In the same enchaînement I designate a rond de jambe en l'air through 90 degrees.

In the adagio section, we develop (in addition to développés and grands ronds de jambe) all variants of fouettés and pirouettes using different methods and proceeding from pose to pose, from développés tombés and flic-flacs en tournant, into the major pose.

I blend doubles battements frappés with petits battements and battements battus, and add vivacity to the movement through spinning and through turns of the torso into small and major poses.

The last movement practised at the barre is the grand battement. It is important that the legs are thrown upward in a light and fast manner.

It is useful to include in the exercise at the barre such jumps as ballonnés battus, cabrioles fermées and cabrioles, ronds de jambe en l'air sautés and grands fouettés sautés en tournant.

The complex movements of the senior grades require a completely different co-ordination of movement than in the junior and middle grades. Starting with the battement tendu, I set various arm movements and turns of the torso. Often I end the movement in poses rather than the 5th position.

At the end of the barre exercise, I consider it extremely useful to set a series of various stretches to develop the stance and suppleness.

The pace of the exercise at the barre should be exceptionally calm. It is vital that every movement be worked through so as to consolidate past training and a constant aspiration for suppleness and absolutely perfect execution. A slow pace affords the opportunity to achieve this.

However, the whole exercise cannot be built on a slow pace. Apart from alternating slow and fast paces, it is useful to perform an enchaînement at a slow pace and then repeat at a faster pace.

I recommend against big pauses between movements during exercises at the barre. We have to remember that one of the aims is to work up muscle strength and stamina. Some teachers stop a lesson to explain mistakes and correct pupils, and they lose much time in the process. Such pauses disturb the flow of any exercise and frustrate the whole purpose of the movements. I consider that the explanations, repetitions and corrections should come in the pause after the completion of the exercises at the barre.

We maintain a traditional approach to the exercises in the centre. A small adagio is the first combination performed in the centre. The pupils are asked to check their steadiness unsupported, especially in movements involving transfers from one leg to the other. They are expected also to make ready for more complex movements.

A small adagio can be arranged perfectly in a temps lié with a pirouette or a grand temps relevé en tournant. It is useful to check out and work up one or two complex movements in the small adagio. We propose a fouetté en effacée or a grand fouetté en tournant into third arabesque and first arabesque. At the first stage they can be combined with various tours lents and pirouettes ending in major poses, and the tours can be gradually made more difficult in the major poses. I invariably join a small adagio with a battement tendu and a turn. The whole enchaînement is repeated in reverse.

The battement fondu is performed in major poses, with turns. Tours are included in the major poses with pliés-relevés. These are performed several times in succession. All this demands and develops good equilibrium.

We devote much attention in the senior grades to turns. The budding ballet dancer must master the technique of turning perfectly if he or she is ever to achieve the heights of expression on the stage. He or she must catch the dynamics and energy of the turn, keeping it smooth and unbroken.

Pirouettes should be a feature of the whole lesson. They require daily practice. Yet if we overdo them, we will not get the required results. Efficiency should be sought, not so much in terms of the number of times each individual movement is practised, as the quality of execution. We are looking for an academically proper and attractive form of pirouette. When working on a turn which travels, a pupil must be taught to distribute the space on the dance floor correctly. He or she must be able to mentally draw out lines – straight, diagonal and circular – and stick to them when performing.

A grand adagio in the senior grades is a small dance study. It usually lasts 32 bars of 3/4 music. The adagio includes a maximum number of complex elements, and requires of students balance, stamina, a good feel for music, and drama. It seems to summarise the all-round readiness of the pupils. This is what makes it so important to consolidate various techniques and work up complex movements in the enchaînements preceding the grand adagio.

A grand battement should feature speed with a lightness of upward thrust of the legs. It should be remembered that a grand battement is performed in the senior grades sur les demi-pointes and using the torso. Usually a grand battement is combined with virtuoso movements such as a grand fouetté en tournant into different poses; or with a complicated spin, leaps, or other steps.

Eminent teachers of choreography have always stressed the importance of the allegro. Vaganova wrote in her *Fundaments of Classical Dance* (Iskusstvo Publishers, Leningrad, 1980, p. 14): 'The allegro contains the whole science of dance, all its complexity; it is an earnest of future refinement.'

In contemporary productions, ballet masters use all forms of jump, seeing them as a vivid expressive means of revealing the main images. The long high jumps are particularly popular today. They are the grand jeté, the jeté entrelacé, the grand jeté pas de chat, and the jeté en tournant in diagonals, circles, etc.

It should be recalled that the most testing jumps are now performed by the players in the corps-de-ballet too, and not just by the ballerinas and soloists. This has caused the choreographic school to devote added attention to grande élévation.

At each lesson all the various jumps – big, small and medium – should be thoroughly worked out.

Let me just recall something N. Tarasov once said: 'Good elevation and flight depend on a pupil having sufficient strength, stamina and willpower . . . The small and insufficient number of jumps included in each task cannot duly affirm good elevation and flight' (N. Tarasov, *Classical Dance*, Iskusstvo Publishers, Moscow, 1971, p. 212).

I recommend that teachers plan jumps for a whole week, making sure each lesson contains at least two enchaînements with small jumps, two with medium jumps, and at least four with big jumps. At least twenty minutes should be given over to this.

The master should explain the difference between the small, medium and big jumps. He should also get the students to sense the difference between low, flat jumps and high, vaulting leaps.

A whole series of jumps such as grande sissonne ouverte, grand jeté renversé, jeté passé and pas de ciseaux can be worked up nicely in the exercises in the centre. They can be blended into enchaînements with adagios and grands battements.

When working on the allegro, it is vital that all the connecting movements be practised, since the quality and vigour of the preparation for the jump assist the dancer in performing the jump itself correctly and well. Careless connecting movements often spoil the general impression of combined jumps, even where the main leaps are well done.

The gliding section for budding ballerinas is no less important than the men's. Apart from mastering the fine points of classical dance, work on glissades develops strength in the legs.

Contemporary ballet shows require perfect control over the toes. A ballet dancer has to perform intricate turns, jumps and transitions between poses up on her pointes. I have at least three lessons sur les pointes every week. But the training is daily. In the centre it is good to practise several enchaînements up on three-quarter pointes, including them in the battement fondu, the adagio, and the grand battement. Consequently, these exercises will develop correct technique for full pointe work.

On days when the exercise sur les pointes is practised, less time is devoted to the centre and allegro. The grand adagio can be left out since it can be partially performed sur les pointes.

The length of the enchaînements with a dance form increases in the senior grades (but they should last no longer than 32 bars of 3/4 music).

The construction of each enchaînement should be conditioned by the task of the whole lesson, and at the same time each enchaînement is inseparably linked with the previous and the ensuing ones.

Tarasov indicated: 'All should be interlinked and everything should work for methodological integration in a lesson. There should be a choreographical and logical elegance of development and not fragmentation into separate, unconnected parts' (Tarasov, p. 82).

Each teacher daily, creating enchaînements, is like a maître de ballet staging a dance composition. As I have mentioned, the ability of the teacher to build enchaînements is of immense significance. There are teachers who get carried away with the idea of maître de ballet (see notes on p. xix), and form enchaînements which do not quite correspond to the curriculum of a particular grade. At the same time, a primitive enchaînement does not develop the pupil's dance abilities and expression.

An enchaînement should be more than useful training. It should develop artistry and feeling, and should assist pupils in developing professional memory and interpretation.

I believe in particular principles for building enchaînements for training. First I compose a fairly simple enchaînement, and gradually make it more complicated as we move from lesson to lesson, going from the simple to the complex. When pupils are tired, I propose less demanding enchaînements, proceeding from the complex to the simple in such cases.

Change of pace within the enchaînement plays a big role. Suppose at the barre we do a rond de jambe à terre. I set 4 bars of 3/4 music as follows – 2 ronds, 3 ronds, 5 ronds and 2 ronds.

When composing an enchaînement one can use logical development of movement or interrupt it with a counter-motion which in music is equivalent to a counter-beat. Such 'inconvenient' enchaînements create extra difficulties for the pupils, instilling agility and control over the whole body.

I feel it proper to use, during lessons, individual steps of variations from classical ballets. These variations were created by the great choreographers of the past, and work on them is good for the artistic individuality of the students.

One should not forget that daily repetition of the same movements engenders automatic execution. Mechanical repetition spoils the whole purpose of a movement.

Regrettably, in our profession quantity does not always beget quality. Good quality can only be attained through conscious work, through constant self-control. Older students should know precisely how and where each movement is performed, and should be able to analyse mistakes. If pupils are taught to think carefully about what they are doing, to check themselves, the teacher does not have to do much talking during movements.

Short corrective remarks suffice. I recommend that teachers use extra-curricular time to show pupils the methodology of classical dance. Such a method of training brings theory and practice together, and yields palpable results.

The musical accompaniment of the lessons in the senior grades is immensely important. Our graduates must be ready to work in the theatre, and there they will meet diverse and sometimes most complex music for ballet. So lessons should feature serious music, Russian and foreign classics, and the best works of Soviet times. The concert master has a big part to play in class. His contact with the teacher is vital.

When drafting a lesson and individual enchaînements, a teacher should proceed not just from the metre and rhythm of the music. He must ably convey its character, and its particular form and structure. Only then can the true musicality be instilled which is such an essential quality for a ballet performer today.

Sophia Golovkina

How To Use This Book

Placing is based on the stage (or studio) being divided into 8 points. Point 1 is centre stage up front.

```
┌─────────────────────┐
│  4      5      6     │
│                     │
│                     │
│  3             7     │
│                     │
│                     │
│  2      1      8     │
└─────────────────────┘
```

The exercises are laid out in four columns. The number of bars required is given before time signature at the beginning of each exercise. The extreme left column shows the order of execution of the exercises. The figure 1 represents the 1st bar; the figure 2 means the 2nd bar. The figures 1–4 mean from the first bar to the fourth. Each set of four bars is divided from the next set by a horizontal line. The second column shows the number of parts in which movement occurs during the bar. The symbol ♩ designates a quarter of a bar, and the symbol ♪ describes one eighth of a bar. 2 ♩ means that the movement extends over two-fourths of a bar. The third column describes the position and movements of the legs. The fourth column applies only to the arms. Thus the words arms and legs do not usually appear in the text. In the third column R (or L) means the right (or left) leg; and in the fourth column R (or L) means the right (or left) arm.

The following abbreviations are used for annotation.

battement	bt
en dedans	en dd
en dehors	en dh
arabesque	arb
right	R
left	L

Here is an example:

Battement tendu

8	3/4	V R devant		R – bras bas
1–2		pause		R – I – II
1	2 ♩	R 2 bts tendus devant		
2	2 ♩	L 2 bts tendus derrière		
3	3 ♪	R 3 bts tendus à la seconde, closing V devant		
4		R bt tendu relevé à la seconde, closing V derrière		
1–4		repeat in reverse		

This is a description of the movement battement tendu in the exercise at the barre. The figure 8 in the far left column indicates the number of bars in the whole exercise. The 3/4 in the second column describes the musical measure. V R devant in the third column means that the 5th position is taken, with the right leg forward. In the 4th column, R – bras bas means the right arm is down. The introduction before the movement takes 2 bars, during which the position of the legs is maintained and the right arm goes through position I into position II. The movement proceeds in the following manner. In the first bar, the right leg does 2 battements tendus forward in 1/4 time. In the second bar, the left leg does 2 battements tendus back in 1/4 time. In the third bar, the right leg does 3 battements tendus to the side in 1/8 time, closing V devant. In the fourth bar the right leg does a battement tendu relevé à la seconde, closing V derrière. Then movements 1 to 4 are repeated in reverse.

It should be noted that the musical annotation is somewhat conditional. Movements such as battement tendu, battement jeté, battement frappé, grand battement, petit battement sur le cou-de-pied, and the allegro movements and exercises sur les pointes stretch beyond the bar line but that moment is not indicated. And there is also the following detail: 3 battements jetés in 1/8 are performed in 2/4 and the last one-eighth is not mentioned because it serves as the beginning of the next battement jeté.

It is taken for granted that the movements at the barre are performed at a side bar facing the audience. So the initial position is considered to be en face and this correspondingly determines all the directions – croisé, effacé, écarté derrière, devant écarté.

The description of the exercise at the barre implies one hand resting on the barre. This detail is not mentioned in the text. It is assumed.

All the positions of the arms and legs are designated by Roman numerals, and the word position is mostly omitted. Under this system of annotation, a leg forward in position IV is slightly bent, except for position IV in the exercise at the barre in the plié combinations when both legs are extended.

The same terms are used in different ways in different countries. There are cases when one term means different motions or one movement is designated by different terms. All this leads to ambiguity in texts and complicates understanding.

In compiling this work, reference was made to the following works:

Joan Lawson, *Ballet Class*, London, 1984
Syllabuses of the Major Examinations, The Royal Academy of Dancing, London, 1969
Kirsten Ralov, *The Bournonville School*, London, 1979
Gail Grant, *Technical Manual and Dictionary of Classical Ballet*, New York, 1950

We had a difficult choice to make in terminology. We needed terms which best fitted the traditions which have formed Russian choreography and at the same time are widespread throughout the world.

This primarily concerned terms for the main movements in classical dance. Take such a movement as raising the leg. It can be performed in only two ways: either by stretching out the leg or by bending. We use in the first instance the French term dégagé en l'air (used by Kirsten Ralov), and describe the second case as développé.

Another important movement is rising fully or partially onto pointes. This too can be done in only two ways: either through shifting the centre of gravity from one foot to the other by stepping or by a coupé, and in both cases the toes touch the ground. Here we use the French term piqué.

Another way of rising on the toes is through the relevé method. It is the same the world over. We use this for sur les demi-pointes in co-ordination with demi-plié and extended legs.

Battement is viewed by us as a movement having two phases – movement *from* an initial position and *back* into an initial position. Take développé devant. The movement begins from a position. The leg moves up through retiré through 90 degrees. The battement développé devant is performed the same way but ends with letting the foot down into a position, i.e. the initial stance.

The French terms for classical dance are viewed as symbols for specific movements and the rules of French grammar on adjectival endings need not necessarily be observed. This particularly applies to the terms croisé, effacé, écarté, tombé, and allongé.

The movements allegro-assemblé, jeté, entrechat-quatre, royale, entrechat-six, entrechat-trois and entrechat-cinq are performed with an épaulement. This detail is omitted in the text.

In this book in the exercises at the barre, in the centre and allegro, only piqué sur la demi-pointe is used. In the annotation the words sur la demi-pointe are omitted. In the exercise sur les pointes, we similarly write piqué instead of piqué sur la pointe. The same principle applies to the relevé.

For turns on the floor with the leg sur le cou-de-pied, we use the term pirouette, and for spins in poses arabesque and attitude, we use the term tour.

The term battement jeté is used in an equivalent way to battement glissé or battement dégagé. The words temps glissé imply sliding on the sole of the foot in any direction in a pose arabesque or attitude.

During the allegro, the term pas de bourrée en avant is used for big leaps. This represents 3 broad steps forward, with the third step providing the push-off (or impetus) into the leap. Another approach to a leap is the wide glissade; it goes by the principle of the jeté fermé finishing in position IV devant.

Editor's notes

Allongé in Soviet schools means the stretching or straightening of the arms and sometimes the straightening of the spine in arabesque. The position gained is not penché where the body bends over the supporting leg (see example, Lesson 1, 7th year, p. 59).

The term ballet-master in the U.S.S.R. usually means the choreographer and those stage directors who rehearse and re-stage ballets which have to be adapted to the size of the stage, company and so on. They can also be teachers.

In the U.S.S.R. 'spin' usually means pirouette en place – how many depends on the speed of the music and the dancer's ability. 'Tour' (in female dance) usually means a single turn.

Dancers should note the use of III position of the arms during pliés, as this stretches the spine into the correct stance during the rise.

The pianist in all senior classes in the U.S.S.R. is known as the concert-master and plays an active part in the lesson.

The Sixth Year of Study

LESSON ONE

The Exercises at the Barre

Plié

80	3/4	I position	Right bras bas (L on the barre)
1–2			R – I – II (L on the barre)
1–4		I position, demi-plié	R – III – II
1–4		R 4 bts tendus à la seconde, closing I (R, L, R, L)	
1–4		grand plié	R – bras bas – I – II
1–3 4		grand plié, finishing R dégagé à terre à la seconde	R – III – I – II

Battement tendu.

1–3 4	II position, demi-plié, finishing R pointe tendue à la seconde	R – III – II
1 2 3 4	transfer weight on R, L pointe tendue transfer weight on L, R pointe tendue transfer weight on R, L pointe tendue transfer weight on L, R pointe tendue	
1–4	II position, grand plié	R – bras bas – I – II
1–3 4	grand plié R demi-rond de jambe à terre en dd, finishing pointe tendue devant	R – III – I – II
1–4	IV position, demi-plié	R – III – II
1–4	4 bts tendus à la seconde R, L, R, L, closing IV devant, derriére . . .	

Port de bras.

1–4	grand plié	R – bras bas – I – II
1–3	grand plié	R – III – I – II
4	close R in V devant	
1–4	V R devant, demi-plié	R – III – II
1–4	4 bts tendus à la seconde R, L, R, L, closing V devant, derrière . . .	

1–4		grand plié	R – bras bas – I – II
1–3		grand plié	R – III – II
4		relevé	
1–7		3rd port de bras sur les demi-pointes,	
8		finishing L retiré, R on the whole foot	
1–2		bend sideways to the left	R – III
3–4		recover	R – II
1		R relevé	
2		pause	
3		close L in V derrière on the whole foot	R – bras bas
4		pause	

Battement tendu

32	2/4	V R devant	R bras bas
1	♩	pause	R – I
	♩		R – II
1	2 ♩	R 2 bts tendus devant	
2	♩	3rd bt tendu through I into dégagé à terre derrière en fondu	
	♩	close R in V derrière, straighten knees	
3–4	4 ♩	L 4 bts tendus devant	R – II
1	2 ♩	R 2 bts tendus derrière	
2	♩	3rd bt tendu through I into dégagé à terre devant en fondu	R – III
	♩	close R in V devant, straighten knees	
3–4	4 ♩	L 4 bts tendus derrière	R – II
1–3	6 ♩	R 6 bts tendus à la seconde, closing V derrière, devant . . ., finishing R dégagé à terre à la seconde	
4	♩	II demi-plié, finishing straighten L, with R pointe tendue à la seconde	R – I – II
	2 ♪	lower R heel twice, stretch pointe tendue	
1–4	16 ♪	R 16 bts tendus à la seconde, each closing I and concluding V R derrière	R – bras bas – I – II
1–16		repeat in reverse close V R devant	

Battement jeté (performed without pause after battement tendu in all lessons)

16	2/4		
1	2 ♩	R 2 bts jetés devant	R – bras bas – I – III
2	3 ♪	R 3 bts jetés devant	
3	2 ♩	L 2 bts jetés derrière	R – I – 1 arb
4	3 ♪	L 3 bts jetés derrière	

Battement retiré.

1–2	4 ♩	L 4 bts retirés sur le cou-de-pied, closing V devant, derrière . . .	R – III – II
3–4	7 ♪	R 7 bts jetés à la seconde, each closing I and concluding V R derrière	R – bras bas – I – II
1–8		repeat in reverse	

Rond de jambe à terre

64	3/4	I position	R – bras bas

Préparation en dehors.

1–2	préparation en dh	R – I – II
1–4	4 ronds à terre en dh	
1	rond à terre en dh, finishing pointe tendue devant	R – I
2	L en fondu hold and R rond à terre en dh, finishing pointe tendue derrière	R – II
3	R rond à terre en dd, finishing pointe tendue devant	
4	demi-plié in I position, straighten L with R dégagé à terre derrière	

1–8	repeat 1–8 bars
1–15	repeat the whole exercise in reverse
16	demi-plié in I position, straighten L with R rond de jambe à terre en dh

Grand rond de jambe jeté en dehors.

1	grand rond de jambe jeté en dh
2	rond à terre en dh
3	grand rond de jambe jeté en dh
4	rond à terre en dh,
1–2	finishing grand bt devant, finishing passé développé derrière R – III – II
3	R through I into dégagé à terre devant
4	R through I into rond de jambe à terre en dd

Grand rond de jambe jeté en dedans.

1–7	repeat 1–8 bars (beginning from grand rond de jambe jeté) in reverse	
8	close V R derrière	R – bras bas
1	L développé devant	R – I – II
2	pause	
3–4	R fondu with bend forwards	R – I
1–2	straighten R, with bend backwards	R – III
3	recover	R – II
4	close L in V devant	R – bras bas
1	R développé derrière	R – I – II
2	pause	
3	L deepen fondu with R pointe tendue derrière	R – 2 arb
4	pause	
1	L holding fondu, rising a little with R dégagé 90° 2nd arb	
2	L relevé	
3	close R in V derrière, bend backwards	
4 2 ♩	recover	
♩	L step en avant into 1st arb à terre	arms – 1 arb

Battement fondu (performed in all lessons at 45° sur les demi-pointes)

32	3/4	V R devant	R – bras bas
1–2		pause	
1–2		R bt fondu devant 45°	R – bras bas – I – II
3		L fondu	
4	2 ♩	1/2 tour en dh with R devant 45°	
	♩		R on the barre, L – II
1–2		L bt fondu derrière 45°	L – bras bas – I – II
3		R fondu	
4	2 ♩	1/2 tour en dd with L derrière 45°	
	♩		L on the barre, R – II
1–2		R bt fondu à la seconde 45°	R – bras bas – I – II
3–4		L fondu and 2 pirouettes en dh, finishing R à la seconde 45°	R – I – II
1–2		L bt fondu devant 90°	R – bras bas – I – III
3–4		R bt fondu à la seconde 90°	R – I – II
1–16		repeat in reverse, finishing R à la seconde 45° sur la demi-pointe	

Battement frappé (performed without pause after battement fondu in all lessons)

8	2/4		
1–2	7 ♪	L 7 bts frappés devant	R – II
	♪	pause	
3–4	7 ♪	R 7 bts frappés derrière	
	♪	pause	
1–2	7 ♪	R 7 bts frappés à la seconde	
	♪	pause	

Préparation from fondu into temps relevé.

3–4		L fondu with R sur le cou-de-pied devant	R – I
		from temps relevé 2 pirouettes en dh, finishing R attitude derrière sur la demi-pointe	R – III

Rond de jambe en l'air

16	2/4	V R devant	R – bras bas
1		préparation – temps relevé en dh	R – I – II

Préparation rond de jambe en l'air en dehors.

1	3 ♪	3 ronds en l'air en dh, finishing en fondu	
	♪	tour fouetté en dh,	
2	♩	finishing R à la seconde 45° sur la demi-pointe	R – II
	♩	double rond en l'air	
3–4		repeat 1–2 bars	
1–2	3 ♪	3 doubles ronds en l'air (en dh, en dd, en dh)	
	♩	L fondu with R sur le cou-de-pied devant	R – I
3		2 pirouettes en dh,	R – II – I
4	♪	finishing close R in V derrière in demi-plié	R – bras bas
	♩	détourné into V R devant	R – I
	♪	R dégagé 45° à la seconde	R – II
1–8		repeat the whole exercise in reverse	

Demi-plié détourné into V.

Adagio

16	3/4	V R devant	R – bras bas
1–2		pause	
1		R développé devant sur la demi-pointe	R – I – II
2		pause	
3–4		demi-rond de jambe, finishing R à la seconde	
1–2	♩	L fondu 2 pirouettes en dh, finishing R attitude derrière	R – III
3		R tombé en arrière, finishing L dégagé 90° devant	R – III allongé
4		bend backwards	
1		L piqué en avant into 2nd arb	R – 2 arb
2		L on the whole foot with bend forward	R – I
3–4		recover with R demi-rond de jambe en dd, finishing à la seconde	R – II
1–2		L fondu and 2 pirouettes en dd, finishing R devant 90° sur la demi-pointe	R – III
3		fouetté, finishing 4th arb	R on the barre, L – 4 arb

Fouetté into 4th arabesque.

| 4 | | close R in V derrière | L – bras bas |

Battement double frappé

16	2/4	V R devant	R – bras bas
1	♩	relevé in V	R – I
	♩	R dégagé 45° à la seconde	R – II
1	♩	bt double frappé sur la demi-pointe, finishing pointe tendue à la seconde	
	♩	repeat the same devant	
2	♩	bt double frappé sur la demi-pointe, turning (1/2) to the left, finishing pointe tendue derrière	R on the barre, L – II
	♩	bt double frappé sur la demi-pointe, turning (1/2) to the right en face, finishing pointe tendue à la seconde	L on the barre, R – II

3–4		R petit bt sur le cou-de-pied (derrière–devant) sur la demi-pointe	R – bras bas – I – II
1		L fondu with R sur le cou-de-pied devant from temps relevé 2 pirouettes en dh, finishing R à la seconde 45°	R – I R – II
2		pause	
3		R bt battu effacé devant	R – I
4	♩	finishing R pointe tendue effacé devant en fondu	
	♩	turning to the left en face, L relevé with R à la seconde 45°	R – II
1–8		repeat in reverse	

Grand battement

32	3/4	V R devant	R – bras bas
1–2		pause	R – I – II
1–2		R 2 grands bts devant	
3–4		3rd through I into grand bt derrière	R – 2 arb
1–4		L 4 grands bts devant	R – II
1–2		R 2 grands bts derrière	
3–4		3rd through I into grand bt devant	R – 2 arb
1–4		L 4 grands bts derrière	
1–4		R 4 grands bts à la seconde closing V derrière, devant . . . sur les demi-pointes	R – II
1		R développé à la seconde en fondu	R – bras bas – I – II
2		1 tour fouetté en dh, finishing R écarté derrière 90° sur la demi-pointe	R – III
3–4		close R in V derrière, turning to the left en face	R – II – bras bas
1–4		R 4 grands bts à la seconde, closing V devant, derrière . . . sur les demi-pointes	R – I – II
1		R développé à la seconde en fondu	R – bras bas – I – II
2		tour fouetté en dd, finishing R écarté devant sur la demi-pointe	R – III
3–4		close R in V devant, turning to the right en face	R – II – bras bas

The Exercises in the Centre

Petit adagio

32	3/4	V R croisé devant	arms – bras bas
1			arms – I
2		V demi-plié	R – I, L – II
1–2		1 pirouette en dh, finishing R croisé devant 90° en fondu	arms – I
3		R piqué en avant to point 8 into attitude croisé derrière	L – III, R – II
4		close L in V derrière, turning to the right (1/8) en face, V R devant in demi-plié	arms – II R – I, L – II

1–2		1 pirouette en dh, finishing R à la seconde 90° en fondu	arms – I – II
3		R piqué de côté to point 3, with L dégagé 90° à la seconde	
4		pause sur la demi-pointe	
1–2		L demi-rond de jambe en dh, finishing attitude croisé derrière on the whole foot	L – III, R – II
3		R relevé	
4		close L in IV derrière with R fondu (préparation for tours en dd)	R – I, L – II
1–2		2 tours en dd in attitude derrière, finishing facing 2	L – III, R – II
3		R fondu with L extended	arms – allongé
4		pas de bourrée en dh into V L croisé devant	arms – II – bras bas
1–16		repeat in reverse	

Battement tendu

8	2/4	V R croisé devant	arms – bras bas
1			
1	2 ♩	turning to the right facing 4, R 2 bts tendus devant	arms – through I to L – III, R – II
2	2 ♩	L 2 bts tendus derrière	arms – allongé
3	2 ♩	turning to the right facing 5 R 2 bts tendus à la seconde, closing V derrière, devant	arms – II
4	2 ♩	turning to the right, en face L 2 bts tendus à la seconde, closing V devant, derrière, finish V R devant in demi-plié	R – I, L – II
1		1 pirouette en dh into IV R croisé derrière (préparation for pirouettes en dh)	arms – I – 3 arb
2		2 pirouettes en dh, into V R croisé derrière	arms – I – bras bas
3	3 ♪	L 3 bts jetés croisé devant	R – I, L – II
4	3 ♪	R 3 bts jetés croisé derrière	arms – 3 arb

Battement fondu

16	3/4	V R croisé devant	arms – bras bas
1–2		pause	
1–2		en face R bt fondu à la seconde 90°	arms – I – II
3	2 ♩	R rond de jambe en l'air en dh finishing effacé devant	R – III, L – II
	♩	R tombé en avant to point 2 into 1st arb	
4		pas de bourrée en dh into V L croisé devant	arms – bras bas
1–4		repeat to the other side, close V R croisé devant	
1–2		en face L bt fondu à la seconde 45°	arms – I – II
3–4		L 3 ronds de jambe en l'air en dh, finishing en fondu	
1–2		pas de bourrée en tournant en dh, finishing L tombé en avant to point 1	L – I, R – II
3		2 pirouettes en dd into V R croisé devant demi-plié	arms – I – bras bas
4		relevé in V	arms – I – III

Grand battement

4	4/4	V R croisé devant	arms – bras bas
1		pause	
1	2 ♩	R 2 grands bts croisé devant	arms through I to L – III, R – II
	♩	3rd grand bt, finishing passé développé derrière in 1st arb	arms – I – 1 arb
	♩	close R in V derrière	
2	2 ♩	R 2 grands bts effacé derrière	
	♩	3rd grand bt, finishing passé développé croisé devant	arms through I to L – III, R – II
	♩	close R in V devant	arms – II
3	3 ♩	en face 3 grands bts à la seconde (R, L, R), closing V derrière	
	♩	pause	
4	3 ♩	3 grands bts à la seconde (L, R, L), closing V derrière, finishing in demi-plié	arms – bras bas
	♩	détourné into V L croisé devant	arms – I – III

Pirouettes

8	2/4	V R croisé devant	arms – bras bas
1		pause	
1		R sissonne tombé effacé en avant, to point 2, pas de bourrée into IV L croisé devant (préparation for pirouette en dh)	arms – I to R – I, L – II arms – 3 arb
2		2 pirouettes en dh into IV R croisé derrière	arms – I – 3 arb
3		R sissonne tombé effacé en avant to point 2 pas de bourrée, finishing L tombé en avant en face	arms – I to R – I, L – II arms – bras bas – I L – I, R – II
4		2 pirouettes en dd into V R croisé devant	
1–4		repeat	

Grand adagio

32	3/4	V R croisé devant	arms – bras bas
1–2		pause	
1–2		R développé effacé devant en fondu	arms – I to L – III, R – II
3		close R in V effacé devant, in demi-plié	arms – II
4		turning to the left facing 8, straighten knees	arms – bras bas
1–2		L développé in 1st arb to point 2 en fondu	arms – I – 1 arb

Arabesque into grand fouetté finishing in attitude.

3		close L in V effacé derrière in demi-plié	arms – II
4		turning to the left facing 8, straighten knees	arms – bras bas
1–2		R piqué en avant to point 8,	arms – I
		L through I into grand fouetté, finishing attitude effacé derrière sur la demi-pointe	L – III, R – II
	♩	L passé petit développé croisé devant en fondu	arms – I
3–4		L piqué en avant to point 2,	
		R through I into grand fouetté, finishing attitude effacé derrière sur la demi-pointe	R – III, L – II
	♩	L fondu with R extended	arms – allongé
1–2		pas de bourrée en dh,	arms – bras bas – I
		finishing R step en avant into 4th arb to point 8	arms – 4 arb
3–4		pause	
1		penché in 4th arb	
2		recover with fouetté, finishing facing 5, L à la seconde 90°	arms – II
3		fouetté (turning to the left), finishing L croisé devant	R – III, L – II
4		pause	
1		R relevé	
2		chassé en avant to point 2, finishing L tombé en avant into wide IV (préparation for tours en dd)	
3–4		2 tours en dd in 1st arb, finishing facing 8	L – I, R – II
1–2		tour lent en dd sur la demi-pointe, finishing facing 8 en fondu	
3		pas de bourrée en dh into V R croisé devant in demi-plié	arms – bras bas
4		en face R relevé with L développé à la seconde	

Grand fouetté en tournant en dedans.

1–2	grand fouetté en tournant en dd, finishing 3rd arb to point 8 en fondu	
3	L passé développé effacé devant	R – III, L – II
4	L step en avant to point 8, finishing R pointe tendue effacé derrière	arms – allongé

Allegro

The First Exercise

16	2/4*	V L croisé devant	arms – bras bas
1	♩	R petit jeté battu dessus	R – I, L – II
	♩	temps levé	
2	♩	L petit jeté battu dessus	L – I, R – II
	♩	temps levé	

*In all allegro exercises the introduction is one bar in 2/4 time.

Petit jeté dessus.

Temps levé.

Assemblé dessus.

3–4	3 ♩	3 assemblés battus dessus (R, L, R)	arms – bras bas
	♩	straighten knees	
1–4		repeat the whole exercise	

Petit jeté dessous.

Assemblé dessous.

1–8		repeat in reverse	

The Second Exercise

16	2/4	V R croisé devant	arms – bras bas
1	♩	jeté fermé en avant to point 8 into 3rd arb, finishing V R croisé devant	arms – I – 3 arb
	♩	straighten knees	
2	♩	entrechat-quatre	arms – I – III
	♩	straighten knees	arms – II
3	♩	jeté fermé en arrière to point 4, finishing V R croisé devant	arms – I to L – III, R – II
	♩	straighten knees	arms – II
4	♩	entrechat-quatre	arms – I – III
	♩	straighten knees	arms – II

Sissonne ouverte en tournant finishing petit développé à la seconde.

1	♪	en face, R double rond de jambe en l'air en dh sauté	arms – I – II
	♪	R assemblé dessous into V croisé derrière	arms – bras bas
2	♪	en face, L double rond de jambe en l'air en dh sauté	arms – I – II
	♪	L assemblé dessous into V croisé derrière	arms – bras bas
3	♪	sissonne ouverte en tournant (to the right), finishing en face R petit développé à la seconde	arms – I – II
	♪	R assemblé dessous into V croisé derrière	arms – bras bas
4	♪	entrechat-quatre, travelling en avant to point 2	arms – I – III
	♪	straighten knees	arms – II – bras bas
1–8		repeat in reverse	

The Third Exercise

8	2/4	V R croisé devant	arms – bras bas

Ballonné dessous.

1–2	4 ♪	facing 2, 4 ballottés sauté en effacé 90° (R devant, L derrière)	L – I, R – II; R – I, L – II
3		L coupé dessous	
		R ballonné dessous	L – I, R – II

4		R step en avant to point 2	arms – I
		grand jeté en avant in attitude croisé derrière	arms – II
1		en face R glissade de côté, finishing V L devant	arms – I
		R ballonné 90° dessus	arms – II allongé
		close R in V devant in demi-plié	R – I, L – II

Ballonné dessus.

2		en face L glissade de côté, finishing V R devant	arms – I
		L ballonné 90° dessus	arms – II allongé
		close L in V devant in demi-plié	L – I, R – II
3	2 ♩	2 sissonnes fermées en avant to points 8, 2 into 2nd arb, changing épaulement, finishing V L croisé devant	
4	♩	soubresaut	arms – I – II
	♩	straighten knees	

The Fourth Exercise

16	3/4*	IV L pointe tendue croisé devant	arms – demi II
1		pause	
2		R wide glissade avant to point 2	arms – I
1–2		grand fouetté sauté, finishing 1st arb on L to point 7	arms – 1 arb
3		L relevé in attitude effacé derrière	arms – I to R – III, L – II
4		failli en avant to point 8	arms – II
		L wide glissade en avant to point 8	arms – I
1–2		grand fouetté sauté, finishing 1st arb on R to point 3	arms – 1 arb
3		R relevé in attitude effacé derrière	arms – I to L – III, R – II
4		failli en avant to point 2	arms – II
		pas de bourrée en avant to point 2	arms – I
1–2		L grand assemblé en avant	arms – III
3		R piqué en avant to point 2 into 1st arb	
4		facing 8, L chassé de côté to point 6	arms – II allongé

*In all allegro exercises the introduction is one bar in 3/4 time.

1–2		R grand assemblé dessus en tournant en dd, finishing V R croisé devant	arms – I – III
3		relevé in V	arms – allongé
4		pause	

The Fifth Exercise

16	3/4	IV L pointe tendue croisé devant	arms – demi – II
1		pause	
2		R wide glissade en avant to point 2	arms – I
1–2		grand jeté en avant in 1st arb onto R	arms – 1 arb
3	2 ♩	pas de bourrée en dh into V L croisé devant sur les demi-pointes	arms – bras bas
	♩	détourné into V R croisé devant	arms – I – III
4		L wide glissade en avant to point 8	arms – II – I
1–2		grand jeté en avant in 1st arb onto L	
3	2 ♩	pas de bourrée en dh into V R croisé devant sur les demi-pointes	arms – bras bas
	♩	détourné into V L croisé devant	arms – I – III
4		pas de bourrée en avant to point 2	arms – II – I
1–2		grand jeté en avant in 3rd arb onto L pas de bourrée en avant to point 2	
3–4		grand jeté en avant in 1st arb onto R pas de bourrée en avant to point 2	
1–2		grand jeté en avant in 3rd arb onto L R glissade de côté, finishing V L devant	
3		R piqué en avant to point 2 into 1st arb	
4		pause	

The Sixth Exercise

8	3/4	V R croisé devant	arms – bras bas
1–2		R sissonne tombé effacé en avant pas de bourrée	arms – I to R – I, L – II
3		R wide glissade en avant to point 2	arms – II – I
4		grand pas de chat, finishing V L croisé devant	R – III, L – I, arms – allongé
1–4		repeat 1–4 bars to the other side to point 7	
1–4		repeat 1–4 bars to point 3	
1–2		2 times pirouette-piqué en dd on L travelling to point 8	
3–4		chaînés, finishing 2nd arb à terre on L	

The Seventh Exercise

8	2/4	V L croisé devant	arms – bras bas
1		R brisé en avant to point 2	arms – I to R – I, L – II
		sissonne simple on L, R sur le cou-de-pied devant	R – III, L – II

Brisé en avant.

2		repeat 1st bar	
3		brisé dessus-dessous to point 2	
4		pas de bourrée en tournant en dh into V R croisé devant	arms – bras bas
		L brisé en avant to point 8	arms – I to L – I, R – II

Brisé dessus-dessous.

1–4		repeat the whole exercise to the other side

The Exercises sur les Pointes

The First Exercise

8	2/4	V R croisé devant	arms – bras bas
1	♩	échappé into IV R devant to point 2, finishing V R croisé devant	arms – 1 arb arms – bras bas
	♩	en face échappé into II, finishing V L croisé devant	arms – demi II arms – bras bas
2	♩	échappé into IV L devant to point 2, finishing V L croisé devant	arms – I – 3 arb
	♩	détourné into V R croisé devant in demi-plié	
3	♩	facing 8, sissonne simple derrière on R, into V R croisé devant	R – I, L – II
	♩	facing 8, sissonne simple devant on L, into V R croisé devant	L – I, R – II

Sissonne simple derrière.

Sissonne simple devant.

4	♩	1 pirouette en dh into V R croisé derrière	arms – I – bras bas
	♩	relevé in V, travelling en avant to point 2	arms I to R – III, L – I arms – allongé
1–4		repeat to the other side	

The Second Exercise

8	2/4	V R croisé devant	arms – bras bas
1	♩	en face, R ballonné relevé dessus	arms – I – demi II – I
	♪	L relevé with R petit développé effacé devant, finishing L fondu	L – I, R – II
2		pas de bourrée en dd into V L croisé devant	arms – bras bas
3	♩	en face L ballonné relevé dessous	arms I – demi II – I
	♩	R relevé with L petit développé effacé derrière, finishing R fondu	arms – 2 arb
4		pas de bourrée en dh into IV (préparation for pirouette en dh)	arms – I – 3 arb
1		2 pirouettes en dh into V R croisé derrière in demi-plié	arms – I – bras bas
2	♩	détourné into V R croisé devant	arms – I – III
	♩	L relevé with petit développé effacé devant, finishing R tombé en avant to point 2	arms – I to R – I, L – II arms – I
3–4	3 ♩	3 relevés into 1st arb on R, travelling en arrière to point 6	
	♩	R relevé with L développé croisé devant, close L in V croisé devant sur les pointes	R – III, L – II

The Third Exercise

32	3/4	V R croisé devant	arms – bras bas
1–2		L relevé with R développé croisé devant, finishing V R croisé devant in demi-plié	arms – I to R – II, L – III arms – bras bas
3–4		R relevé into 3rd arb to point 8, finishing V R croisé devant in demi-plié	
1–2		R piqué en avant to point 8 L through I into grand fouetté, finishing attitude effacé derrière en fondu	arms – I L – III, R – II
3–4		pas de bourrée en dh, finishing R fondu with L petit développé croisé devant	arms – bras bas
1–2		L piqué en avant to point 2 L through I into grand fouetté, finishing attitude effacé derrière en fondu	arms – I R – III, L – II
3–4		pas de bourrée en dh into wide IV (préparation for tour en dd)	arms I to R – I, L – II
1–2		tour en dd in attitude derrière on L, finishing facing 8 en fondu	L – III, R – II arms – allongé
3–4		pas de bourrée en dh into V R croisé devant in demi-plié	arms – bras bas
1–32		repeat in reverse	

The Fourth Exercise

8	2/4	V R croisé devant	arms – bras bas
1	♩	pause	
	♪	L fondu with R petit développé effacé devant	arms – I
	♪	R tombé en avant to point 4	
1–2	3 ♩	3 relevés into 1st arb, turning to the right to points 4, 6, 8	arms – 1 arb
	♩	facing 8, R relevé with L développé effacé devant	arms – I to R – III, L – II

3	♩	L tombé–relevé with R petit développé croisé devant	L – III, R – II
	♩	R tombé–relevé with L petit développé effacé devant	R – III, L – II
4	♩	L tombé–relevé with R petit développé croisé devant	L – III, R – II
	♪	close R in V croisé devant in demi-plié	arms – II – bras bas
	♪	relevé in V	arms – I – III
1–4		repeat to the other side	

The Fifth Exercise

| 4 | 2/4 | IV L devant en face (préparation for tours en dh) | arms – 3 arb |
| 1–4 | 8 ♩ | 8 tours en dh on L with R attitude devant, finishing IV R croisé derrière | arms – II |

The Sixth Exercise

8	2/4	V R croisé devant	arms – bras bas
1	2 ♪	2 sautés sur les pointes into V	arms – I with wrists crossed allongé
	♩	L fondu on the whole foot with R petit développé croisé devant	R – I, L – II
2	♩	emboîté sauté on R with L sur le cou-de-pied derrière L coupé dessous	arms – demi II allongé
	♩	R assemblé dessous into V L croisé devant	arms – bras bas
3–4		repeat 1–2 bars to the other side, close V R croisé devant	
1	3 ♪	3 sautés sur la pointe on L in attitude effacé devant, facing 2	arms – demi II allongé
	♪	L fondu (on the whole foot)	
2	♩	L relevé with R petit développé écarté devant	
	♪	facing 8, close R in V croisé devant in demi-plié	
	♪	relevé in V	arms – bras bas
3	4 ♪	4 sautés sur la pointe on R in attitude croisé derrière	arms – I to L – III, R – II
4	♩	close L in V croisé derrière in demi-plié	arms – bras bas
	♩	détourné into V L croisé devant	arms – I – III

The Seventh Exercise

8	2/4	IV R pointe tendue croisé devant en diagonale from point 6 to point 2	R – I, L – II
1–2	4 ♩	4 times pirouette-piqué en dd on R,	
3–4		chaînés	
1–2	4 ♩	4 times posé pirouette-piqué en dh on L	
3–4		chaînés, finishing 2nd arb à terre on R	

The Eighth Exercise

| 8 | 2/4 | IV L devant en face (préparation for pirouettes) | arms – 3 arb |
| 1–8 | 16 ♩ | 16 tours fouettés, finishing IV R croisé derrière | arms – II |

LESSON TWO

The Exercises at the Barre

Plié

80	3/4	I position	R – bras bas
1–2		pause	R – I – II
1–4		I position, grand plié	R – bras bas – I – II
1–4		grand plié	R – III – I – II
1–3		3 relevés (without demi-plié)	
4		pause sur les demi-pointes	
1–2			arms – II
3		I position on the whole foot	L on the barre
			R – bras bas – I – II
4		R dégagé à terre à la seconde	
1–4		II position, grand plié	R – bras bas – I – II
1–4		grand plié	R – III – I – II
1		relevé	arms – 2 arb
2		pause	
3–4		bend backwards	L on the barre
1–2		recover	
3		II position on the whole foot	
4		R demi-rond de jambe à terre en dd finishing pointe tendue devant	R – II
1–4		IV position, grand plié	R – bras bas – I – II
1–4		grand plié	R – III – I – II
1		relevé	
2–3		bend sideways to the left	R – III
4		recover	R – II
1–2		turning to the left (1/2) in IV position sur les demi-pointes, finishing IV L devant	R on the barre, L – II
3–4		IV position, on the whole foot	L – bras bas – I – II
1–4		IV position, grand plié	L – bras bas – I – II
1–4		grand plié	L – III – I – II
1		relevé	
2–3		bend sideways to the right	L – III
4		recover	L – II
1–2		turning to the right (1/2) in IV position sur les demi-pointes, finishing IV R devant	L on the barre, R – II
3		IV position on the whole foot	
4		close R in V devant	R – bras bas – I – II
1–4		V position, grand plié	R – bras bas – I – II
1–4		grand plié	R – III – I – II
1–2	♩	relevé with bend forward	R – bras bas – I – III
3		recover	

4		R retiré	
1–2		bend backwards	R – II
3		recover	
4		close R in V devant, on the whole foot	R – bras bas

Battement tendu

16	2/4	V R devant	R – bras bas
1			R – I – II
1	2 ♩	R 2 bts tendus devant	
2	♩	3rd bt tendu through I into dégagé à terre derrière	R – III
	♩	demi-rond de jambe à terre en dd, finishing pointe tendue à la seconde	R – I – II
3–4	4 ♩	4 bts tendus à la seconde, closing V devant, derrière . . .	
1	2 ♩	R 2 bts tendus derrière	
2	♩	3rd bt tendu through I into dégagé à terre devant	R – III
	♩	demi-rond de jambe à terre en dh, finishing pointe tendue à la seconde	R – II
3–4	4 ♩	4 bts tendus à la seconde, closing V derrière, devant . . .	
1	2 ♩	2 bts tendus à la seconde, closing V derrière, devant . . .	
2		R dégagé à terre à la seconde demi-rond de jambe à terre en dh, finishing pointe tendue derrière pause	R – 2 arb
3–4	4 ♩	4 bts tendus derrière	
1	2 ♩	2 bts tendus à la seconde, closing V devant, derrière . . .	R – II
2		R dégagé à terre à la seconde demi-rond de jambe à terre en dd, finishing pointe tendue devant pause	R – III
3–4	4 ♩	4 bts tendus devant	R – II

Battement jeté

24	2/4		
1	2 ♩	R 2 bts jetés devant	R – III
2	3 ♪	3 bts jetés devant	
3	2 ♩	2 bts jetés à la seconde, closing V derrière, devant . . .	R – I – II
4	3 ♪	3 bts jetés à la seconde, closing V derrière, devant, derrière . . .	
1	2 ♩	2 bts jetés derrière	R – 2 arb
2	3 ♪	3 bts jetés derrière	
3–4	4 ♩	4 petit bts développés en croix, close V L devant	R – 2 arb – II – III – II
1–8		repeat the whole exercise in reverse	
	♪	close R dégagé 45° à la seconde	
1		R flic-flac en tournant en dh, finishing R devant 45°	R – II
2	3 ♪	3 bts jetés piqués devant,	
	♪	finishing demi-rond de jambe 45° dh	

3	3 ♪	3 bts jetés piqués à la seconde,	
	♪	finishing demi-rond de jambe 45° en dh	
4	3 ♪	3 bts jetés piqués derrière,	
	♪	close V derrière	
1–4		repeat 1–4 bars (beginning flic-flac) in reverse	

Rond de jambe à terre

64	3/4	I position	R – bras bas
1–2		préparation en dh	R – I – II
1–3		3 ronds à terre, finishing dégagé 45° devant	R – bras bas – I
4		rond de jambe 45°	R – II
1–8		repeat twice 1–4 bars	
1–2		3 ronds à terre, finishing pointe tendue devant	
3–4		3 ronds à terre, finishing pointe tendue devant	
1–16		repeat the whole exercise (1–16 bars) in reverse	
1		grand rond de jambe jeté, close V derrière	
2		bt tendu à la seconde, close V devant	
3–6		repeat twice 1–2 bars	
7		grand bt devant,	R – I – III
		finishing passé développé derrière	R – II
8		through I into dégagé à terre devant	
1–8		repeat 1–8 bars (starting grand rond de jambe jeté)	
		in reverse, close V R devant	R – bras bas
1		R développé devant sur la demi-pointe	R – I – II
2		tombé en avant, finishing L pointe tendue derrière	
3		bend backwards	R – I – III
4		recover, close L in V derrière, straighten knees	R – II – bras bas
1		L développé derrière sur la demi-pointe	R – I – II
2		tombé en arrière, finishing R pointe tendue devant	
3		bend backwards	R – I – III
4		recover, close R in V devant, straighten knees	R – II – bras bas
1		R développé à la seconde sur la demi-pointe	R – I – II
2		tombé de côté, finishing L pointe tendue à la seconde	arms – II
3		bend sideways to the right	L – III, R – II
4		recover	arms – II
1		L piqué de côté with R dégagé 90° à la seconde	L on the barre, R – II
2		bend sideways to the left	R – III
3		recover	R – II
4		close R in V devant, on the whole foot	R – bras bas

Battement fondu

16	3/4	V R devant	R – bras bas
1–2		pause	

1–2	R bt fondu devant 45°	R – I – II
3	demi-rond de jambe en dh, finishing à la seconde en fondu	
4	tour fouetté en dh, finishing à la seconde 45° sur la demi-pointe	R – I – II
1–2	L bt fondu devant 90°	R – bras bas – I – III
3–4	R bt fondu à la seconde 90°	R – I – II
1–8	repeat in reverse, finishing R à la seconde 45° sur la demi-pointe	

Battement frappé

8	2/4		
1–2	7 ♪	R 7 bts frappés à la seconde	R – II
	♪	R tombé dessus, L sur le cou-de-pied derrière	R – I

Tombé dessus.

Tombé dessous.

| 3 | ♩ | L coupé dessous, R ballonné dessous | R – II – I |
| | ♩ | L relevé with R petit développé à la seconde | R – II |

27

4	3 ♪	R 3 bts frappés à la seconde	
	♪	pause	
1–4		repeat in reverse	

Rond de jambe en l'air

16	2/4	V R devant	R – bras bas
1		préparation – temps relevé en dh	R – I – II
1	3 ♪	3 ronds en l'air en dh, rising gradually to 90°	R – bras bas – I – III
	♪	pause	
2	2 ♩	2 ronds en l'air 90° en dh	
3	2 ♩	2 ronds en l'air 90° en dd	
4	3 ♪	3 ronds en l'air en dd, falling gradually to 45°	
	♪	pause	
1–2	4 ♩	4 doubles ronds en l'air (en dh, en dd, en dh, en dd)	
3	♩	L fondu with R sur le cou-de-pied devant	R – I
	♩	from temps relevé 2 pirouettes en dh, finishing à la seconde 45° sur la demi-pointe	R – I – II
4		close R in V derrière sur les demi-pointes	R – bras bas
		détourné into V R devant	R – I
		R dégagé 45° à la seconde sur la demi-pointe	R – II
1–8		repeat in reverse	

Adagio

32	3/4	V R devant	R – bras bas
1–2		pause	
1		R développé devant on the whole foot	R – I
2–4		grand rond de jambe, finishing 2nd arb	R – II – 2 arb
	♩	L fondu with R retiré	R – I
1–4		L holding fondu, R grand rond de jambe, finishing 2nd arb	R – II – 2 arb
	♩	L relevé with R retiré	R – I
1–4		L holding sur la pointe, R grand rond de jambe, finishing 2nd arb	R – II – 2 arb
	♩	R retiré	R – I
1		R développé devant	R – III
2		tombé en avant, finishing L dégagé 90° derrière	R – III allongé
3		L through I into grand fouetté relevé, finishing L derrière 90°	L – III allongé, R on the barre
4		close L in V derrière	L – II – bras bas
1–16		repeat with L foot in reverse	

Battement double frappé

16	2/4	V R devant	R – bras bas
1	♩	relevé in V	R – I
	♩	R dégagé 45° à la seconde	R – II
1	♩	bt double frappé sur la demi-pointe, finishing pointe tendue croisé devant on the whole foot	R – III
	♩	demi-rond de jambe à terre en dh, turning to the left, en face	R – II
2	3♪	3 bts doubles frappés à la seconde sur la demi-pointe	
	♪	pause	
3	♩	bt double frappé sur la demi-pointe, finishing pointe tendue croisé derrière on the whole foot	R – III
	♩	demi-rond de jambe à terre en dd, turning to the right, en face	R – II
4	3♪	3 bts doubles frappés à la seconde sur la demi-pointe	
	♪	pause	
1–2		R petit bt sur le cou-de-pied (derrière–devant) sur la demi-pointe	R – bras bas – I – II
3		R tombé dessus, L sur le cou-de-pied derrière L coupé dessous, 1 pirouette en dh, finishing à la seconde 45° sur la demi-pointe	R – II
4	3♪	R bt battu effacé devant	R – I
	♪	turning to the left en face, R à la seconde 45°	R – II
1–8		repeat in reverse, close 2nd arb à terre	

Grand battement

32	3/4	V R devant	R – bras bas
1–2			R – I – II
1		grand bt devant	
2		2nd grand bt, finishing passé développé derrière	R – 2 arb
3–4		grand bt piqué derrière, close V derrière	
1–4		repeat in reverse	R – III
1–4		4 grands bts à la seconde, closing V derrière, devant . . . sur la demi-pointe, close on the whole foot	R – I – II R – bras bas
1		bt développé effacé devant sur la demi-pointe, close on whole foot	R – I – III
2		turning to the left, en face, bt développé à la seconde sur la demi-pointe, close V derrière on whole foot	R – I – II
3		bt développé effacé derrière sur la demi-pointe, close on the whole foot	R – 2 arb
4		turning to the right, en face, bt développé à la seconde sur la demi-pointe, close V derrière on whole foot	R – II
1–16		repeat the whole exercise in reverse	

The Exercises in the Centre

Petit adagio

32	3/4	V R croisé devant	arms – bras bas
1–2		pause	

Grand temps relevé en tournant en dehors.

1–2	R grand temps relevé en tournant en dh (1/2) (to the right), finishing facing 5	arms I – II
3–4	close R in V devant, on the whole foot	arms – bras bas
1–2	L grand temps relevé en tournant en dd (1/2) (to the right), finishing en face en fondu	arms – I – II
3–4	pas de bourrée en dd, finishing en face L fondu, R retiré devant	L – I, R – II
1	R grand temps relevé en tournant en dh (to the right),	
2	finishing en face en fondu	arms – II
3–4	pas de bourrée en tournant en dh into wide IV R croisé devant (préparation for tours en dd)	arms – I R – I, L – II

1–2		2 tours en dd à la seconde on R, finishing en fondu	arms III – II
3–4		pas de bourrée en dh into V L croisé devant	arms – bras bas
1–16		repeat in reverse with other foot	

Battement tendu

16	2/4	V R croisé devant	arms – bras bas
1			
1–2	4 ♩	R 4 bts tendus effacé devant	arms – I to L – III, R – II
3–4	4 ♩	L 4 bts tendus effacé derrière	arms – allongé
1–2	4 ♩	en face 4 bts tendus à la seconde (R, L, R, L), closing V derrière	arms – I – II
3–4	5 ♪	R 5 bts jetés à la seconde, closing I	
	3 ♪	R dégagé 45° à la seconde	
1		R flic-flac en tournant en dh, finishing R croisé devant 45° sur la demi-pointe	
		R tombé en avant into IV (préparation for pirouettes en dd)	R – I, L – II
2		2 pirouettes en dd into V L croisé devant	arms – I – bras bas
3–4		en face 4 bts tendus à la seconde (L, R, L, R), closing V derrière	arms – I – II
1–2	5 ♪	L 5 bts jetés à la seconde, closing I	
	3 ♪	L dégagé 45° à la seconde	
3		L flic-flac en tournant en dh, finishing L croisé devant 45° sur la demi-pointe	
		L tombé en avant into IV (préparation for pirouettes en dd)	L – I, R – II
4		2 pirouettes en dd into V R croisé devant	arms – I – bras bas

Battement fondu

32	3/4	V R croisé devant	arms – bras bas
1		relevé	arms – I
2		R dégagé 45° à la seconde sur la demi-pointe	arms – II
1–4		R 4 ronds de jambe en l'air en tournant en dh (to the right) to point 3, 5, 7, 1 sur la demi-pointe, finishing R effacé devant 45° en fondu	R – I, L – II
1–2		on R tour-piqué en dd in attitude derrière, finishing point 2 en fondu with L extended	L – III, R – II arms – allongé
3–4		pas de bourrée en dh, finishing R fondu with L sur le cou-de-pied devant	arms – bras bas – I L – I, R – II
1–2		on L tour-piqué en dd in attitude derrière, finishing point 8 en fondu with R extended	R – III, L – II arms – allongé
3–4		pas de bourrée en dh into V R croisé devant sur les demi-pointes	arms – bras bas
1–2		R bt fondu effacé devant 90°	arms – I to R – III, L – II
3–4		L bt fondu effacé derrière 90° (in 1st arb)	arms – 1 arb
		close L in V croisé devant sur les demi-pointes en face R dégagé 45° à la seconde	arms – bras bas – I – II
1–16		repeat in reverse	

Pirouettes

8	2/4	IV R pointe tendue croisé devant en diagonale from point 6 to point 2	R – I, L – II
1–2 3–4	4 ♩	4 times pirouette-piqué en dd on R chaînés	
1–4		repeat, close 2nd arb à terre on R	

Grand adagio

32	3/4	V R croisé devant	arms – bras bas
1–2		L fondu with R dégagé à terre croisé devant demi-plié in IV, transfer weight on R, L pointe tendue croisé derrière (straighten R)	arms – I L – III, R – II
1–2 3–4		facing 8, relevé with closing L V derrière pas de bourrée suivi without travelling in V R croisé devant L fondu with R dégagé à terre croisé devant demi-plié in IV, transfer weight on R, L pointe tendue croisé derrière (R straighten)	 arms – 4 arb arms – I L – III, R – II
1–4		6th port de bras, finishing IV R croisé devant (préparation for tours en dd)	R – I, L – II
1–2 3–4		2 tours en dd in attitude derrière, finishing point 2 pause	L – III, R – II
1–2 3 4		tour lent en dd, finishing point 8 in 3rd arb R fondu L step en arrière, close R in croisé devant	 arms – bras bas
1 2–3 4		R développé croisé devant grand rond de jambe, finishing effacé derrière sur la demi-pointe close R in V croisé devant	arms – I to R – III, L – II arms – allongé arms – bras bas
1 2 3–4		en face R développé à la seconde R close II in demi-plié 2 tours en dh in à la seconde on L, finishing en face	arms – I – II R – I, L – II arms – III
1–2 3 4		R passé développé effacé devant en fondu R piqué en avant to point 2 into 1st arb R on the whole foot	arms – II – I arms – 1 arb
1–2 3 4		penché in 1st arb recover close L in V croisé devant	 arms – bras bas

Sixth port de bras.

Grand battement

16	3/4	V R croisé devant	arms – bras bas
1–2		pause	arms – I to L – III, R – II
1–2		R 2 grands bts croisé devant, close in demi-plié	
3		jeté fermé en avant to point 8 into V R croisé devant	arms – I – 3 arb
4		straighten knees	
1–2		L 2 grands bts croisé derrière, close in demi-plié	
3		jeté fermé en arrière to point 4 (facing 8) into V R croisé devant	arms – I to L – III, R – II
4		straighten knees	
1–2		L 2 grands bts écarté derrière, closing V derrière, devant . . .	
3–4		R 2 grands bts écarté devant, closing V derrière, devant . . .	R – III, L – II
1–3		en face 3 grands bts à la seconde (L, R, L), closing V devant	arms – II
4		pause	

Allegro

The First Exercise

16	2/4	V R croisé devant	arms – bras bas
1	♩	L petit jeté battu dessus	L – I, R – II
	♩	R assemblé dessus	arms – bras bas
2	♩	L petit jeté battu dessus	L – I, R – II
	♩	R assemblé dessus	arms – bras bas
3	♩	en face, sauté in V R devant	R – I, L – II
	♩	2 pirouettes en dh on L into V R croisé derrière in demi-plié	arms – I – bras bas
4	♩	relevé	
	♩	pause	
1–4		repeat with the other foot	
1–8		repeat the whole exercise in reverse	

The Second Exercise

8	2/4	V R croisé devant	arms – bras bas
1	♩	en face R double rond de jambe en l'air en dh sauté	arms – I – II
	♩	R assemblé dessous into V croisé derrière	arms – bras bas
2	♩	sissonne fermée en avant to point 2 into 3rd arb, finishing V L croisé devant	arms – 3 arb
	♩	straighten knees	arms – bras bas
3–4		repeat with other foot	

1	2 ♩	2 sissonnes fermées en avant to points 3, 7 into 2nd arb, finishing V croisé devant, changing épaulement	arms – I – 2 arb
2	♩	gargouillade en dh (R, L), finishing V L croisé devant	arms – I – II
	♩	straighten knees	arms – bras bas
3	2 ♩	2 sissonnes fermées en avant to points 7, 3 into 2nd arb, finishing V croisé devant, changing épaulement	
4	♩	gargouillade en dd (R, L), finishing V R croisé devant	arms – I – II – bras bas
	♩	changement de pied	arms – I – II

The Third Exercise

16	3/4	V R croisé devant	arms – bras bas
1		en face échappé into II	arms – I – II
2		from II grande sissonne ouverte en avant to point 3 into 1st arb on R	arms – 1 arb
3–4		pas de bourrée en dh into V L croisé devant	arms – bras bas
1		en face, échappé into II	arms – I – II
2		from II grande sissonne ouverte en arrière to point 6 on L with R effacé devant	L – III, R – II
3–4		pas de bourrée en dd into V L croisé devant	arms – bras bas
1–2		en face R glissade de côté, closing V L devant R grand assemblé battu dessus, finishing V R croisé devant	arms – II – I R – III, L – II, arms – allongé
3–4		en face L glissade de côté, closing V R devant L grand assemblé battu dessus, finishing V L croisé devant	arms – II – I L – III, R – II, arms – allongé
	♩	relevé	L – I, R – II
1–4		chaînés to point 8, finishing 2nd arb à terre on L	

The Fourth Exercise

8	2/4	IV L pointe tendue croisé devant	arms – demi II
1		en face R glissade de côté, finishing V L devant R cabriole effacé devant	arms – I L – III, R – II
2	3 ♪	3 emboîtés on R, L, R (sur le cou-de-pied derrière), turning to the left facing 8	arms – II – bras bas
3		en face L glissade de côté, finishing V R devant L cabriole effacé devant	arms – II – I R – III, L – II
4	3 ♪	3 emboîtés on L, R, L (sur le cou-de-pied derrière)	arms – II – bras bas
1–2		repeat 1–2 bars, without turning	
3	♪	L coupé dessous R step en arrière to point 6 into 1st arb en fondu	
	3 ♪	3 temps glissés into 1st arb, travelling en arrière to point 6	

Failli into 4th arabesque à terre.

4	♩	R relevé
	♩	failli into 4th arb à terre on L to point 2

The Fifth Exercise

16	3/4	IV L pointe tendue croisé devant en diagonale from point 6 to point 2	arms – demi II
1		pause	
2		pas de bourrée en avant to point 2	arms – II – I
1–2		grand jeté en avant in attitude croisé derrière on L	R – III, L – II
		pas de bourrée en avant	arms – II – I
3–4		grand jeté en avant in attitude croisé derrière on L	R – III, L – II
		R sissonne tombé effacé en avant	R – I, L – II
1–2		pas de bourrée en dd,	arms – bras bas
3		finishing R piqué en avant into 1st arb	arms – I – 1 arb
4		facing 8, L chassé de côté to point 6	arms – II allongé

Failli into 4th croisé derrière.

1–2		R grand assemblé dessus en tournant, finishing V R croisé devant	arms – I – III
3	2 ♩	grande sissonne ouverte en avant to point 2 into 2nd arb on R	arms – 2 arb
	♩	R relevé	
4		facing 8, L chassé de côté to point 6	arms – II allongé
1–2		R grand assemblé dessus en tournant, finishing V R croisé	arms – I – III
3	2 ♩	grande sissonne ouverte en avant to point 2 into 2nd arb on R	arms – 2 arb
	♩	R relevé	
4		failli into IV R pointe tendue croisé derrière	arms – I to R – III, L – II

The Sixth Exercise

8	3/4	IV L pointe tendue croisé devant en diagonale from point 6 to point 2	arms – demi II
1			
2		R wide glissade en avant to point 2	arms – I
1–2		grand pas de chat	R – III, L – I, arms – allongé
		R wide glissade en avant	arms – II – I
3–4		repeat twice 1–2 bars	
7–8		R sissonne temps levé 1st arb running to point 2	arms – I – 1 arb

Sissonne temps levé into 1st arabesque.

The Seventh Exercise

8	2/4	V L croisé devant	arms – bras bas
1	♩	R brisé dessus to point 2	R – I, L – II
	♩	L through I into attitude effacé derrière sur la demi-pointe	L – III, R – II
2	♩	failli	arms – II
	♩	pas de chat	arms – I – III

Failli.

3–6		repeat twice 1–2 bars	
7	2 ♩	brisé dessus-dessous to point 2	
8	♩	pas de bourrée en tournant en dh into V R croisé devant	arms – bras bas
	♩	soubresaut	arms – I – III

The Exercises sur les Pointes

The First Exercise

8	2/4	V L croisé devant	arms – bras bas
1	♩	échappé into IV L devant to point 2, finishing V L croisé devant	arms – I to R – I, L – II
	♩	échappé into II, turning to the right facing 5, finishing V L devant	arms – bras bas arms – demi II
2	♩	échappé into IV L devant, turning to the right (1/8) facing 6, finishing V L devant	arms – I – 3 arb
	♩	échappé into II, turning to the right, en face, finishing V L croisé devant	arms – demi II
3	♩	R relevé with L petit développé croisé devant, finishing V R croisé devant in demi-plié	R – I, L – II
	♩	L relevé with R petit développé croisé derrière, finishing L fondu with R sur le cou-de-pied derrière	arms – 3 arb
4	♩	1 pirouette en dh into V R croisé devant in demi-plié	arms – I – bras bas
	♩	relevé in V	arms – demi II
1–4		repeat to the other side	

The Second Exercise

8	2/4	V R croisé devant	arms – bras bas
1	♩	facing 8, sissonne simple devant on L, into V R croisé devant	R – I, L – II
	♩	L relevé with R double rond de jambe en l'air en dh, finishing V R croisé derrière, changing épaulement	arms – bras bas
2	♩	facing 2, sissonne simple devant on R into V L croisé devant	L – I, R – II
	♩	R relevé with L double rond de jambe en l'air en dh, finishing V L croisé derrière, changing épaulement	arms – bras bas
3	♩	R ballonné relevé effacé devant	arms – I to L – I, R – II
	♩	L relevé with R petit développé écarté derrière, finishing V R croisé derrière in demi-plié	arms – demi II allongé arms – bras bas
4	♩	détourné into V R devant in demi-plié en face	R – I, L – II
	♩	2 pirouettes en dh into V R croisé derrière	arms – I – bras bas
1–4		repeat to the other side	

The Third Exercise

16	3/4	V R croisé devant	arms – bras bas
1		L relevé with R développé effacé devant	arms – I to R – III, L – II
2		R tombé en avant to point 2 into 1st arb	arms – 1 arb
3–4		pas de bourrée en dh into V L croisé devant in demi-plié	arms – bras bas
1	2 ♩	facing 2 L relevé with R développé écarté derrière	arms – I to R – III, L – II
	♩	L fondu	
2	2 ♩	fouetté relevé, finishing attitude effacé derrière on L	
	♩	L fondu	arms – allongé
3–4		pas de bourrée en dh, finishing L fondu with R petit développé croisé devant	arms – I – bras bas
1		R piqué en avant to point 8 into 4th arb	arms – I – 4 arb
2–3		2 relevés in 1st arb, turning to the right, finishing facing 2	
4		failli into IV L croisé devant (préparation for pirouettes en dd)	L – I, R – II
1–2		2 pirouettes en dd into V R croisé devant in demi-plié	arms – III
3		relevé in V	arms – I to L – III, R – I, arms – allongé
4		pause	

The Fourth Exercise

8	2/4	V R croisé devant	arms – bras bas
1	2 ♩	L 2 relevés with R attitude croisé devant	arms – I with wrists crossed
2	♪	L relevé with R développé écarté devant	R – III, L – II
	♪	R tombé dessus, L sur le cou-de-pied derrière	arms – II
	♪	L glissade de côté to point 6, finishing V R croisé devant	
	♪	L petit jeté de côté, finishing R sur le cou-de-pied devant	arms – bras bas
3–4		repeat 1–2 bars	

1	4 ♪	4 emboîtés piqués en tournant en dd to point 2 (on R, L, R, L) with sur le cou-de-pied devant	
2		chaînés	
3	4 ♪	repeat 4 emboîtés	
4		chaînés, finishing 2nd arb à terre on R	

The Fifth Exercise

8	2/4	V R croisé devant	arms – bras bas
1	♩	R relevé into 1st arb to point 2, finishing V L croisé devant in demi-plié	arms – I – 1 arb arms – bras bas
	♩	L relevé into attitude croisé derrière, finishing V L croisé devant in demi-plié	arms – I to R – III, L – II
2	3 ♪	3 temps levés sur la pointe on R with L attitude croisé devant, finishing V L croisé devant in demi-plié	arms – II – bras bas
3–4		repeat with other foot	
1	♩	R relevé into 1st arb to point 2, finishing V L croisé devant in demi-plié	arms – I – 1 arb arms – bras bas
	♩	L relevé into attitude croisé derrière, finishing V L croisé devant in demi-plié	arms – I to R – III, L – II
2	♩	détourné into V R croisé devant	arms – II – I – III
	♩	facing 8, L step de côté to point 6 with R pointe tendue croisé devant	arms – II to R – I, L – II
3–4	4 ♩	4 times posé pirouette en dh on L, finishing IV R croisé derrière	arms – 3 arb

The Sixth Exercise

8	2/4	IV R pointe tendue croisé devant en diagonale from point 6 to point 2	R – I, L – II
1–2	3 ♩	3 times pirouette-piqué en dd on R	
	2 ♪	2 chaînés	
5–8		repeat 3 times 1–2 bars, finishing 2nd arb à terre on R	

The Seventh Exercise

8	2/4	IV L devant en face (préparation for pirouette en dh)	arms – 3 arb
1–8	16 ♩	16 tours fouettés, finishing IV R croisé derrière	arms – II

LESSON THREE

The Exercises at the Barre

Plié

104	3/4	I position	R – bras bas
1–2		pause	R – I – II
1–4		I position, grand plié	R – bras bas – I – II
1–4		grand plié	R – III – II
1		relevé	
2		pause	
3		R retiré	R – bras bas – I
4		pause	
1–2		R développé à la seconde	R – II
3		L on the whole foot with R pointe tendue à la seconde	R – bras bas
4		II position	R – I – II
1–4		II, grand plié	R – bras bas – I – II
1–4		grand plié	R – III – II
1		relevé	
2		pause	
3–4		L on the whole foot with R pointe tendue à la seconde	
1–2		demi-rond de jambe à terre en dd, finishing pointe tendue devant	
3		IV position	R – bras bas
4		pause	R – I – II
1–4		IV, grand plié	R – bras bas – I – II
1–3		grand plié	R – III – II
4		relevé	
1–2		bend sideways to the left	R – III
3		recover	R – II
4		L retiré	
1		sur la demi-pointe 1/2 pirouette en dh,	L – I, R on the barre
2		finishing L développé devant sur la demi-pointe	L – II
3		R on the whole foot with L pointe tendue devant	L – bras bas
4		IV position	L – I – II
1–4		IV, grand plié	L – bras bas – I – II
1–3		grand plié	L – III – II
4		relevé	
1–2		bend sideways to the right	L – III
3–4		recover	L – II
1		L retiré	
2		pause	
3		close L in V devant on the whole foot	L – bras bas
4		pause	L – I – II
1–4		V position, grand plié	L – bras bas – I – II

1–3		grand plié	L – III – II
4		relevé	
1–7		3rd port de bras sur les demi-pointes,	
8		finishing R retiré	L – II (see illustration, p. 2)
1		sur la demi-pointe 1/2 pirouette en dh,	R – I
2		finishing pause	L on the barre
3		close R in V devant on the whole foot	R – bras bas
4		pause	R – I – II
1–4		V position, grand plié	R – bras bas – I – II
1–3		grand plié	R – III – II
4		relevé	
1–7		3rd port de bras sur les demi-pointes in reverse,	
8		finishing L retiré	R – II
1–2		pause	
3		close L in V derrière on the whole foot	R – bras bas
4		pause	

Battement tendu

32	2/4	V R devant	R – bras bas
1		pause	R – I – II
1–3	6 ♩	R 6 bts tendus devant	
4	♪	7th bt tendu through I into dégagé à terre derrière	
	♪	fouetté à terre, finishing R pointe tendue devant	R on the barre, L – II
	♩	close R in V devant	
1–3	6 ♩	L 6 bts tendus derrière	
4	♪	7th bt tendu through I into dégagé à terre devant	
	♪	fouetté à terre, finishing L pointe tendue derrière	L on the barre, R – II
	♩	close L in V derrière	

Fouetté à terre.

1	2 ♩	R 2 bts tendus à la seconde, closing V derrière, devant . . .	
2		R bt tendu pour batterie, finishing pointe tendue à la seconde	
3–6		repeat 1–2 bars (bts tendus à la seconde and pour batterie) twice	
7–8	8 ♩	R 8 bts tendus à la seconde, each closing I, and concluding V derrière	R – bras bas – I – II

| 1–16 | | repeat in reverse, close V R devant | |

Battement jeté

16	2/4		R – II
1–3	6 ♩	R 6 bts jetés devant	
4	♪	7th bt jeté through I into dégagé 45° derrière	
	♪	fouetté relevé, finishing R devant 45° sur la demi-pointe	R on the barre, L – II
	♩	close R in V devant on the whole foot	

Fouetté relevé.

1–3	6 ♩	L 6 bts jetés derrière	
4	♪	7th bt jeté through I into dégagé 45° devant	
	♪	fouetté relevé, finishing L derrière 45° sur la demi-pointe	L on the barre, R – II
	♩	close L in V derrière on the whole foot	
1	2 ♩	L 2 bts retirés, closing V devant, derrière . . .	R – III
2	3 ♪	R 3 bts jetés à la seconde, closing V derrière, devant, derrière . . .	R – III
3–4		R 8 bts jetés à la seconde, closing I and V (alternating) close V derrière	

1		flic-flac en tournant en dh, finishing à la seconde 45° on the whole foot	
2	4 ♪	4 bts jetés piqués à la seconde, finishing à la seconde 45°	
3		flic-flac en tournant en dd, finishing à la seconde 45°	
4	3 ♪	3 bts jetés piqués à la seconde, close V derrière	R – bras bas

Rond de jambe à terre

48	3/4	I position	R – bras bas
1–2		préparation en dh	R – I – II
1–2		2 ronds à terre	
3		3 ronds à terre,	
4		finishing pointe tendue devant, rond à terre,	
1		finishing grand rond de jambe jeté	
2		rond à terre	
3		grand rond de jambe jeté,	
4		finishing pointe tendue devant	
1–8		repeat 1–8 bars	
1–16		repeat the whole exercise in reverse, close V R derrière	
1–2		R développé à la seconde	R – bras bas – I – II
3		bend sideways to the left	R – III
4		recover	R – II
1–2		demi-rond de jambe en dd, finishing devant 90° en fondu bend forwards	R – III
3–4		recover, R passé développé derrière with L straightened	R – 2 arb
1–2		R pointe tendue derrière, bend backwards	
3–4		recover	
1–2		R dégagé 90° derrière	
3		L relevé	
4		pause	

Battement fondu

16	3/4	V R devant	R – bras bas
1–2			
1–2		R bt fondu 45° devant	R – I – II
3		through I into dégagé 45° derrière en fondu	
4		fouetté relevé, finishing R devant 45° sur la demi-pointe	R on the barre, L – III
1		L fondu	
2		1/2 tour en dd, R devant 45°	L on the barre, R – II
3–4		R bt fondu à la seconde	R – bras bas – I – II
1–8		repeat the whole exercise in reverse, finishing R à la seconde 45° sur la demi-pointe	

Battement frappé

16	2/4		
1		pause	
1–2	6 ♪	R 6 bts frappés devant sur la demi-pointe, finishing en fondu	R – bras bas – I – III
	♪	R assemblé devant	
	♪	relevé in V	

3–4	6 ♪	L 6 bts frappés derrière sur la demi-pointe, finishing en fondu	R – 1 arb
	♪	L assemblé derrière	
	♪	relevé in V	
1–2	8 ♪	R 8 bts frappés écarté derrière	R – I – III
3	♩	close R V derrière in demi-plié	R – II
	♩	détourné into V R devant in demi-plié	R – I
4		2 pirouettes en dh, finishing à la seconde 45° sur la demi-pointe	R – II
1–8		repeat in reverse	

Rond de jambe en l'air

8	2/4	V R devant	R – bras bas
1		préparation – temps relevé	R – I – II
1	3 ♪	3 ronds en l'air en dh, finishing en fondu	
	♪	pause	
2		2 pirouettes en dh, finishing à la seconde 45° sur la demi-pointe	
3	3 ♪	3 ronds en l'air en dh, gradually rising to 90°	R – bras bas – I – III
	♪	pause	
4	♩	double rond en l'air en dh 90°	
	♪	close R in V derrière sur les demi-pointes	R – II
	♪	détourné, finishing R dégagé 45° à la seconde sur la demi-pointe	
1–4		repeat in reverse	

Adagio

16	3/4	V R devant	R – bras bas
1–2			
1		R développé à la seconde sur la demi-pointe	R – I – II
2		pause	
3	♩	demi-rond de jambe en dd – en dh	
	2 ♩	pause	
4		pause	
1–2		flic-flac en tournant en dh, finishing R attitude devant sur la demi-pointe	R – III
	♩	L fondu	
3–4		grand rond de jambe sur la demi-pointe, finishing derrière en fondu	R – II
1–2		2 pirouettes en dh, finishing R écarté derrière 90°	R – III
3–4		R 2 doubles ronds en l'air en dh 90°	
1–2		turning to the left (1/8) en face, R passé développé devant	R – I – II
3		fouetté, finishing 4th arb sur la demi-pointe	R on the barre, L – 4 arb
4	2 ♩	pause	
	♩	close R in V derrière on the whole foot	

Battement double frappé

16	2/4	V R devant	R – bras bas
1	♩	relevé in V	R – I
	♩	R dégagé 45° à la seconde	R – II
1–2	4 ♩	R 4 bts doubles frappés en croix sur la demi-pointe, finishing pointe tendue	R – I – III
3–4	4 ♩	4 bts doubles frappés à la seconde sur la demi-pointe	
1–2		petit bt sur le cou-de-pied (derrière–devant)	
3–4		bt battu effacé devant, finishing à la seconde 45°, turning to the left (1/2) en face	R – I R – II
1–2	4 ♩	4 bts doubles frappés en croix in reverse sur la demi-pointe, finishing pointe tendue	R – I – III
3–4	4 ♩	4 bts doubles frappés à la seconde sur la demi-pointe	
1–2		L fondu with R sur le cou-de-pied devant from temps relevé 2 pirouettes en dh, finishing R attitude derrière	R – I R – III
3		pause	arms – III
4		close R in V derrière on the whole foot	L on the barre, R – II – bras bas

Grand battement

16	2/4	V R devant	R – bras bas
1–2			R – I – II
1–3	6 ♩	R 6 grands bts devant sur la demi-pointe	
4	♩	7th grand bt through I into grand fouetté, finishing R devant 90° sur la demi-pointe	R on the barre, L – III
	♩	close R in V devant	
1–3		L 6 grands bts derrière sur la demi-pointe	L – II
4	♩	7th grand bt through I into grand fouetté en dd, finishing L derrière 90° sur la demi-pointe	L on the barre, R – III
	♩	close L in V derrière on the whole foot	

Grand fouetté en dedans.

1–3	5 ♩	R 5 grands bts à la seconde, closing V derrière, devant . . ., finishing V derrière in demi-plié	R – II R – bras bas
	♩	détourné into V R devant	
4		R bt développé à la seconde sur la demi-pointe close V R derrière on the whole foot	R – I – II
1–4		repeat the last 1–4 bars	

The Exercises in the Centre

Petit adagio

16	3/4	V L croisé devant	arms – bras bas
1–2		pause	
1		R piqué de côté to point 3, turning to the left (1/4), finishing facing 8, L attitude effacé devant 45° en fondu	arms – demi II allongé R – I, L – II
2		grand fouetté en dh en effacé, finishing R fondu	R – III – II, L – III

Grand fouetté en dehors.

3–4		pas de bourrée en dh into IV L croisé devant (préparation for pirouettes en dh)	arms – 3 arb
1–2		2 pirouettes en dh, finishing attitude croisé derrière	R – III, L – II
3		R passé développé écarté derrière	
4		close R in V derrière	arms – II – bras bas
1–8		repeat in reverse	

Battement tendu

16	2/4	V R croisé devant	arms – bras bas
1		pause	
1–3	6 ♩	R 6 bts tendus croisé devant	arms – I to R – III, L – II
4	♪	7th bt tendu through I into dégagé à terre derrière	
	♪	fouetté à terre, finishing R pointe tendue devant, facing 4	L – III, R – II
	♩	close R in V devant	

1–3	6 ♩	facing 4, L 6 bts tendus derrière	
4	♪	7th bt tendu through I into dégagé à terre devant	
	♪	fouetté à terre, finishing R pointe tendue croisé derrière	arms – 4 arb
	♩	close L in V derrière	
1–2		en face, 4 bts tendus à la seconde (R, L, R, L), closing V derrière	arms – I – II
3–4		R 7 bts jetés à la seconde, each closing I	
		close 8th devant in demi-plié	R – I, L – II
1		2 pirouettes en dh into IV R croisé derrière	arms – I – 3 arb
2		pause	
3		2 pirouettes en dh into V R croisé derrière in demi-plié	arms – I – bras bas
4		détourné into V R croisé devant	arms – I – III

Battement fondu

32	3/4	V croisé devant	arms – bras bas
1–2		pause	
1–2		R bt fondu effacé devant 90°	arms – I to R – III, L – II
3–4		R tombé en avant to point 2, tour en dd in attitude derrière, finishing facing 2	L – III, R – II
1–2		L bt fondu effacé derrière 90°	arms – I – 1 arb
3–4		L tombé en arrière and tour en dh with R devant 90°, finishing facing 2	L – III, R – II
1–2		en face R bt fondu à la seconde 45°	arms – bras bas – I – II
3		3 ronds en l'air en dh, gradually rising to 90°, finishing en fondu	
4		fouetté relevé, finishing 1st arb to point 7 sur la demi-pointe	arms – 1 arb
1–2		pas de bourrée en dh into wide IV R croisé devant (préparation for tours en dh)	arms – I – 3 arb
3–4		2 tours en dh in attitude derrière on R, finishing facing 8	arms – III
1–16		repeat with other foot in reverse	

Pirouettes

8	2/4	V L croisé devant	arms – bras bas
1	♩		
	♩	en face échappé into IV L devant (préparation for pirouettes)	arms – I – 3 arb
1–4	7 ♩	7 tours fouettés, finishing V R devant en face	
	♩	échappé into IV R devant	arms – I – 3 arb
1–4		repeat with other foot	

Grand adagio

32	3/4	V R croisé devant	arms – bras bas
1–2		pause	arms – I – II
1–2		grand plié	arms – bras bas to R – I, L – II
3–4		from deep plié R relevé into attitude effacé derrière	L – III, R – II

1–2		tour lent en dd, finishing facing 2	
3		R relevé with L extended	arms – allongé
4		failli into 4th arb to point 2 en fondu	arms – 4 arb
1–2		pas de bourrée en tournant en dh into wide IV R croisé devant (préparation for tours en dd)	arms – I R – I, L – II
3–4		2 tours en dd with L devant 90°, finishing facing 2 close V L croisé devant	R – III, L – II arms – bras bas
1		en face R développé à la seconde sur la demi-pointe	arms – I – II allongé
2		grand fouetté en tournant en dh, finishing R croisé devant en fondu, facing 8	L – III, R – II
3		L relevé	
4		R tombé en avant into IV R croisé devant (préparation for pirouettes en dh)	arms – 3 arb
1–2		2 pirouettes en dh, finishing 3rd arb à terre to point 8 en deep fondu	arms – I – 3 arb
3		facing 8, L step en arrière to point 4, finishing R pointe tendue croisé devant	arms – I to R – II, L – III
4		pause	
1–2		bend backwards	
3–4		recover	L – II
1	2 ♩	R développé croisé devant sur la demi-pointe	arms – bras bas – I to L – III, L – II
	♩	R tombé en avant to point 8	
2		chassé en avant,	
3		finishing R tombé en avant into wide IV R croisé devant (préparation for tours en dd)	R – I, L – II
4		pause	
1		tour en dd in 1st arb on R, finishing facing 2 en fondu	arms – 1 arb
2		repeat tour	
3–4		pas de bourrée en dh, finishing 4th arb à terre on L to point 2	arms – I – 4 arb

Grand battement

16	3/4	V R croisé devant	arms – bras bas
1–2			
1		grande sissonne ouverte into 1st arb on R, turning to the right facing 4	arms – I – 1 arb
2		L assemblé derrière	
3–4		facing 4, L 2 grands bts derrière	
1		grande sissonne ouverte, turning to the right, facing 8 travelling en arrière to point 4, finishing on L with R croisé devant	arms – I to L – III, R – II
2		R assemblé devant	
3–4		R 2 grands bts croisé devant	
1–3		en face 3 grands bts à la seconde (R, L, R), closing V derrière	arms – II
4		pause	

1–2		R glissade de côté to point 3, finishing V L devant	arms – I
		R grand assemblé battu dessus, finishing V R croisé devant	R – III, L – II, arms – allongé
3–4		en face L glissade de côté to point 7, finishing V R devant	arms – II – I
		L grand assemblé battu dessus, finishing V L croisé devant	L – III, R – II, arms – allongé

Allegro

The First Exercise

8	2/4		V L croisé devant	arms – bras bas
1–2	3 ♩		3 assemblés battus dessus (R, L, R)	
	♩		straighten knees	
3–4	3 ♩		3 assemblés battus dessus (L, R, L)	
	♩		straighten knees	
1			en face échappé into II, finishing L fondu with R sur le cou-de-pied devant, facing 8	arms – I – II – I
2	♩		grand jeté, in 3rd arb on R to point 8	arms – 3 arb
	♩		L assemblé derrière	arms – bras bas
3–4	3 ♩		3 entrechat-quatre	
	♩		straighten knees	

The Second Exercise

16	2/4		V R croisé devant	arms – bras bas
1	♩		R sissonne tombé en tournant (to the right), finishing croisé en avant to point 8	arms – I to R – I, L – II
	♩		L assemblé derrière	arms – bras bas
2	♩		R sissonne tombé en tournant (to the right), finishing de côté to point 3	arms – I – II
	♩		L assemblé dessus into V croisé devant	arms – bras bas
3–4			repeat to the other side with L foot	
1	♩		en face sissonne ouverte, finishing R petit développé à la seconde	arms – I – II
	♩		R double rond de jambe en l'air en dh sauté	
2	♩		R assemblé dessous into V croisé derrière	arms – bras bas
	♩		straighten knees	
3	♩		en face sissonne ouverte, finishing L petit développé à la seconde	arms – I – II
	♩		L double rond de jambe en l'air en dh sauté	
4	♩		L assemblé dessous into V croisé derrière	arms – bras bas
	♩		straighten knees	
1–8			repeat in reverse	

The Third Exercise

16	3/4	V L croisé devant	arms – bras bas
1		en face R grand jeté de côté, to point 3,	arms – I
		finishing L passé développé effacé devant (jeté passé)	R – III, L – II
		2 steps en avant to point 8 (L, R)	arms – II
2		en face L grand jeté de côté to point 7,	arms – I
		finishing R passé développé effacé devant	L – III, R – II
		2 steps en avant to point 2 (R, L)	arms – II
3	♩	en face R grand jeté de côté to point 3,	R – III, L – II
		finishing L passé développé effacé devant (jeté passé)	
	2 ♩	en face L glissade sur les demi-pointes de côté,	
		finishing V L croisé devant	R – I, L – II
4		pause	
1		grand jeté en avant to point 3 in 2nd arb on R	arms – I – 2 arb
		en face L glissade de côté to point 7, finishing V R devant	arms – demi II – I
2		repeat grand jeté and glissade to the other side on L foot	
3		R glissade sur les demi-pointes en tournant en dd to point 4,	arms – I – III
		finishing V R croisé devant	
4		pause	
1–8		repeat the whole exercise to the other side	

The Fourth Exercise

8	2/4	V R croisé devant	arms – bras bas
1	♩	R sissonne tombé croisé en avant to point 8	arms – I
	♩	cabriole in 3rd arb on R	arms – 3 arb
2	♩	L assemblé derrière	arms – bras bas
	♩	straighten knees	
3	♩	L sissonne tombé croisé en arrière to point 4	arms – I
	♩	R cabriole croisé devant on L	L – III, R – II
	♩	R assemblé devant	arms – bras bas
	♩	straighten knees	
1–2	4 ♩	4 petits jetés en tournant to the right (1/2), every half turn,	
		travelling de côté to point 3 (on R, L, R, L)	
3	4 ♪	4 emboîtés sautés en tournant en dd to point 2 (on R, L, R, L)	
		with sur le cou-de-pied devant	
4	3 ♪	chaînés to point 2, finishing V R croisé derrière in demi-plié	arms – I
	♪	relevé in V	arms – II

The Fifth Exercise

16	3/4	IV L pointe tendue croisé devant	arms – demi II
1			
2		R wide glissade en avant to point 2	arms – I
1–2		grand fouetté sauté, finishing 1st arb on L to point 7	
		facing 8, R glissade de côté to point 2,	
		finishing V R croisé devant	arms – I
3	2 ♩	R piqué de côté into attitude croisé derrière	R – III, L – II
	♩	R fondu	

4		pas de bourrée en avant to point 8	arms – II – I
1–2		grand jeté en avant in attitude croisé derrière onto R	L – III, R – II
	♩	L step en avant	
3		grand jeté en avant in attitude croisé derrière onto R	arms – I – II
	♩	L step en avant	
4		grand jeté en avant in attitude croisé derrière onto R	arms – I – II
1		L piqué en avant to point 8 into 1st arb	arms – I – 1 arb
2		facing 2, R chassé de côté to point 4	arms – II allongé
3–4		L grand assemblé dessus en tournant en dd, finishing V L croisé devant	arms – I – III
1		L piqué en avant to point 8 into 1st arb	arms – I – 1 arb
2		facing 2, R chassé de côté to point 4	arms – II allongé
3–4		L grand assemblé dessus en tournant en dd, finishing V L croisé devant	arms – I – III
	♩	relevé in V	arms – allongé

The Sixth Exercise

16	3/4	IV L pointe tendue croisé devant	arms – demi II
1–2		L step en avant to point 2 grand fouetté sauté, finishing facing 7 on L with R extended	arms – I to R – III, L – II, arms – allongé
		failli sauté	arms – II – I
3–4		grand fouetté sauté, finishing facing 3 on R with L extended	L – III, R – II, arms – allongé
		failli sauté	arms – II – I
1–2		grand fouetté sauté, finishing facing 7 on L with R extended	R – III, L – II, arms – allongé
3		pas de bourrée en dh into IV R pointe tendue croisé devant	arms – II – I – II
4		L wide glissade en avant to point 8	arms – I
1–2		grand pas de chat,	L – III, R – I, arms – allongé
		finishing on R with L sur le cou-de-pied derrière, facing 8	R – III, L – II
3		pas de bourrée en tournant en dh into IV L pointe tendue croisé devant	arms – I – II
4		R wide glissade en avant to point 2	arms – I
1–2		grand pas de chat,	R – III, L – I, arms – allongé
		finishing on L with R sur le cou-de-pied derrière, facing 2	L – III, R – II
3		pas de bourrée en tournant en dh into IV R croisé devant (préparation for pirouettes en dh)	arms – I – 3 arb
4		2 pirouettes en dh into IV L croisé derrière	arms – I – II

The Seventh Exercise

8	2/4	V R croisé devant	arms – bras bas
1	♩		
	♩	relevé	arms – demi II allongé

1	♩	demi-plié	
	♩	entrechat-six, finishing facing 2, V L croisé devant	arms – I – III
2		détourné into V R croisé devant	
3	2 ♩	brisé dessus-dessous to point 8	
4	♩	pas de bourrée en tournant en dh into V L croisé devant in demi-plié	arms – I – bras bas
		relevé in V	arms – demi II allongé
1–4		repeat with other foot	

The Exercises sur les Pointes

The First Exercise

8	2/4	V R croisé devant	arms – bras bas
1	♩	facing 8, échappé into II, finishing demi-plié in II	arms – demi II allongé
	♩	L relevé with R sur le cou-de-pied devant, finishing V R croisé devant in demi-plié	L – I, R – II arms – bras bas
2	♩	échappé into II, finishing demi-plié in II	arms – demi II allongé
	♩	R relevé, with L sur le cou-de-pied derrière, finishing V L croisé derrière in demi-plié	R – I, L – II arms – bras bas
3	♩	sissonne simple devant on L into V R croisé devant	R – I, L – II
		L relevé with R double rond de jambe en l'air en dh, finishing V R croisé derrière, facing 2	
4	2 ♩	2 sissonnes simples devant on L en tournant	R – I, L – II, arms – allongé
		en dh to points 6 and 2, into V devant, derrière . . .	arms – bras bas
1–4		repeat with other foot	

The Second Exercise

8	2/4	V L croisé devant	arms – bras bas
1	♩	facing 2, R ballonné relevé dessous (écarté derrière)	L – I, R – II
	♩	facing 8, R ballonné relevé dessus (écarté devant)	arms – demi II allongé
2		pas de bourrée suivi en avant to point 8 in V R croisé devant	arms – 1 arb
3–4		repeat with other foot	
1–2	4 ♩	4 relevés in 1st arb on R, turning to the right to points 4, 6, 8, 2, finishing attitude effacé derrière en fondu	arms – I – 1 arb L – III, R – II, arms – allongé
3		pas de bourrée en dh into IV L croisé devant (préparation for pirouettes en dh)	arms – I – 3 arb
4		2 pirouettes en dh into IV R croisé derrière	arms – I – II

The Third Exercise

16	3/4	V R croisé devant	arms – bras bas
1		L piqué de côté to point 7, turning to the right (1/4) facing 2, finishing R attitude croisé devant 45° en fondu	arms – demi II allongé L – I, R – II

2	2 ♩	grand fouetté en effacé, finishing on L fondu	L – III – II, R – III
	♩	R extended	arms – allongé
3–4		pas de bourrée en dh into V R croisé devant	
1		R piqué de côté to point 3, finishing L attitude effacé derrière 45° en fondu, facing 2	arms – demi II allongé L – I, R – II
2		grand fouetté en effacé, finishing L effacé devant 90° en fondu	arms – II allongé to R – III, L – II
3–4		pas de bourrée en dd into wide IV R croisé devant (préparation for tours en dd)	arms – I to R – I, L – II
1		tour en dd à la seconde on R, finishing en face	arms – II
2		en fondu	
3–4		L soutenu en tournant en dd into V R croisé devant	arms – I – III
	♩	R tombé en avant to point 2	R – I, L – II
1		tour en dd in 1st arb on R	arms – 1 arb
2		finishing facing 2 en fondu	
3–4		pas de bourrée en dh, finishing 4 arb à terre on L to point 2	arms – I – 4 arb

The Fourth Exercise

16	3/4	V R croisé devant	arms – bras bas
1		pause	
2		relevé in V	arms – I to L – III, R – II
1–2		R 2 grands bts croisé devant, close in demi-plié	
3		R relevé with L développé croisé derrière	arms – I – 3 arb
4	♩	close L in V derrière in demi-plié	arms – bras bas
	2 ♩	en face L glissade de côté to point 7, finishing V R devant	arms – demi II allongé – bras bas
1		R relevé with L développé à la seconde	arms – I – III – II
2	♩	close L in V devant in demi-plié	arms – bras bas
	2 ♩	R glissade de côté to point 3, finishing V L devant	arms – demi II allongé – bras bas
3		L relevé with R développé à la seconde	arms – I – III – II
4		close R in V devant in demi-plié	arms – bras bas
1		L through I into grand fouetté relevé into 1st arb to point 3	arms – I – 1 arb
2		R relevé in 1st arb	
3		R relevé in attitude effacé derrière	L – III, R – II
4		failli	
1		R through I into grand fouetté relevé into 1st arb to point 7	arms – I – 1 arb
2		L relevé in 1st arb	
3		L relevé in attitude effacé derrière	R – III, L – II
4		failli into 3rd arb à terre on R to point 8	arms – 3 arb

The Fifth Exercise

8	2/4	IV L pointe tendue croisé devant en diagonale from point 6 to point 2	arms – demi II

1	♩	L piqué en avant with R double bt frappé, finishing L fondu with R pointe tendue effacé devant	L – I, R – II
	♩	R piqué en avant with L double bt frappé, finishing R fondu with L pointe tendue croisé devant	R – I, L – II
2		repeat	
3		pas couru sur les pointes en avant,	
	♪	finishing L fondu with pointe tendue effacé devant	R – I, L – II
4		pas de bourrée en dd into IV L devant en face (préparation for pirouettes en dh)	arms – I – 3 arb
1–4		8 tours fouettés, finishing IV R croisé derrière	arms – II

The Sixth Exercise

8	2/4	V R croisé devant	arms – bras bas
		en diagonale from point 6 to point 2	
1	4 ♩	4 emboîtés piqués en tournant en dd (on R, L, R, L), sur la cou-de-pied devant	
2	♩	R glissade sur les pointes en tournant en dd	
	2 ♪	2 chaînés	
3–8		repeat 3 times, finishing 1st arb à terre on R	

The Seventh Exercise

8	2/4	V R croisé devant	arms – bras bas
1	♩	facing 8, échappé into IV R croisé devant, finishing V R croisé devant	arms – I – 4 arb
	♩	en face, échappé into II, finishing V L croisé devant	arms – I – demi II allongé – bras bas
2	3 ♪	facing 2, 3 temps sautés sur les pointes in V L croisé devant	arms – I to L – III, R – II
3	3 ♪	3 temps levés sur la pointe on L with R attitude croisé derrière	
4	3 ♪	3 temps levés sur la pointe on R with L attitude croisé devant, finishing V L croisé devant on the whole foot in demi-plié	R – III, L – II arms – bras bas
1–4		repeat to the other side	

The Eighth Exercise

8	2/4	IV R pointe tendue croisé devant	R – I, L – II
		en diagonale from point 6 to point 2	
1	2 ♩	2 times pirouette-piqué en dd on R	
2	2 ♪	2 chaînés	
	♩	pirouette-piqué en dd on R	
3–8		repeat 3 times, finishing 1st arb à terre on R	

The Ninth Exercise

8	2/4	IV L devant en face	
		(préparation for pirouettes en dh)	2 arms – 3 arb
1–8	16	16 tours fouettés, finishing IV R croisé derrière	arms – II

The Seventh Year of Study

LESSON ONE

The Exercises at the Barre

Plié

80	3/4	I position	R – bras bas
1–2		pause	R – I – II
1–4		I position, demi-plié	R – bras bas – I
1–4		demi-plié	R – II
1–4		grand plié	R – bras bas – I – II
1–3		grand plié,	R – bras bas – I – III
4		finishing R dégagé à terre à la seconde	R – II
1–4		II position, demi-plié	R – bras bas – I
1–4		demi-plié	R – II
1–4		grand plié	R – bras bas – I – II
1–3		grand plié	R – bras bas – I – III
4		R demi-rond de jambe à terre en dd, finishing pointe tendue devant	R – II
1–4		IV position, demi-plié	R – bras bas – I
1–4		demi-plié	R – II
1–4		grand plié	R – bras bas – I – II
1–3		grand plié	R – bras bas – I – III
4		close R in V devant	R – II
1–4		V position, demi-plié	R – bras bas – I
1–4		demi-plié	R – II
1–4		grand plié	R – bras bas – I – II
1–3		grand plié	R – bras bas – I – III
4		relevé	R – II
1–7		3rd port de bras sur les demi-pointes,	
8		finishing demi-détourné into V L devant	R on the barre, L – II
1–4		V position, demi-plié	L – bras bas – I
1–4		demi-plié	L – II
1–4		grand plié	L – bras bas – I – II
1–3		grand plié	L – bras bas – I – III
4		relevé	L – II
1–7		3rd port de bras sur les demi-pointes in reverse,	
8		finishing demi-détourné into V R devant	L on the barre, R – II

Battement tendu

16	2/4	V R devant	R – bras bas
1		pause	
1–4	7 ♩	R 7 bts tendus effacé devant, closing in demi-plié	R – I – III
	♩	L dégagé à terre derrière, straighten R	R – III allongé
1–4	7 ♩	L 7 bts tendus effacé derrière, closing in demi-plié	
	♩	R dégagé à terre écarté derrière, straighten L	R – III
1–4	7 ♩	R 7 bts tendus écarté derrière, closing V derrière, devant . . . close V derrière in demi-plié	R – II
	♩	détourné into V R devant	
1–4	8 ♪	R 8 bts tendus à la seconde, each closing I, and concluding V devant	R – bras bas – I – II

Battement jeté

16	2/4		
1	2 ♩	R 2 bts jetés devant	R – II
2	3 ♪	3 bts jetés devant	
	♪	dégagé 45° devant, finishing demi-rond de jambe 45° en dh	
3	2 ♩	2 bts jetés à la seconde, closing V devant, derrière . . .	
4	3 ♪	3 bts jetés à la seconde, closing V devant, derrière, devant . . .	
	♪	dégagé 45° à la seconde, finishing demi-rond de jambe 45° en dh	
1	2 ♩	2 bts jetés derrière	
2	3 ♪	3 bts jetés derrière	
	♪	dégagé 45° derrière	
3–4	6 ♪	6 bts jetés balançoirs, closing V derrière	
		pause	
1–8		repeat in reverse	

Rond de jambe à terre

56	3/4	I position	R – bras bas
1–2		préparation en dh	R – I – II
1–3		3 ronds à terre, finishing pointe tendue devant en fondu	R – I
4		turning to the right (1/2) straighten L with R demi-rond à terre en dh, finishing pointe tendue à la seconde	R on the barre, L – II
1–3		3 ronds à terre, finishing pointe tendue devant en fondu	
4		turning to the right (1/2), straighten L with R demi-rond à terre en dh, finishing pointe tendue à la seconde	L on the barre, R – II
1–3		3 ronds à terre, finishing pointe tendue devant en fondu	R – I
4		turning to the right (full turn), straighten L with R rond à terre en dh, finishing pointe tendue devant	arms – I L on the barre, R – II
1		3 ronds à terre	
2–3		2 grands ronds de jambe jetés,	
4		finishing pointe tendue devant	

1–16		repeat in reverse, close V L devant	
1		L développé devant	R – bras bas – I – II
2		pause	
3–4		bend forwards	R – III
1		recover	
2		bend backwards	
3		recover	R – II
4		close L in V devant	R – bras bas
1–2		R développé derrière	R – I – II
3–4		pause	
1–2		penché	R – I
3–4		recover	R – III
1–2		bend backwards	
3–4		recover	R – II
1–4		close R in V derrière	R – bras bas

Battement fondu

32	3/4	V R devant	R – bras bas
1–2		R bt fondu devant	R – I – II
3		L fondu, 1 pirouette en dh, finishing R devant 45°	
4		pause sur la demi-pointe	arms – I with wrists crossed on the chest
1–2		L bt fondu derrière	L on the barre, R – I – II
3		R fondu, 1 pirouette en dd, finishing L derrière 45°	
4		pause sur la demi-pointe	arms – I with wrists crossed on the chest
1–2		R bt fondu à la seconde	L on the barre, R – I – II
3–4		L fondu, 2 pirouettes en dh, finishing à la seconde 45°	
1–4		R 4 bts fondus en croix	
1–16		repeat in reverse, finishing R à la seconde 45° sur la demi-pointe	

Battement frappé

8	2/4		
1–2	7 ♪	7 bts frappés à la seconde	R – II
	♪	close R in V devant in demi-plié	R – I
3		1 pirouette en dh, finishing à la seconde 45° sur la demi-pointe	R – II
4		3 bts frappés à la seconde	
1–4		repeat in reverse	

Rond de jambe en l'air

32	3/4		V R devant	R – bras bas
1–2			pause	
1			R développé devant sur la demi-pointe	R – I
2			demi-rond de jambe en dh, finishing à la seconde	R – II
3			rond de jambe en l'air en dh 90°	
4	♩		R retiré	
	2 ♩		close R in V derrière on the whole foot	R – bras bas
1			R développé derrière sur la demi-pointe	R – I
2			demi-rond de jambe en dd, finishing à la seconde	R – II
3			rond de jambe en l'air en dd 90°	
4	♩		R retiré	
	2 ♩		close R in V devant on the whole foot	R – bras bas
1			R dégagé 90° à la seconde sur la demi-pointe	R – I – II
2–3			2 doubles ronds de jambe en l'air en dh 90°	
4	♩		R retiré	
	2 ♩		close R in V devant on the whole foot	R – bras bas
1			R dégagé 90° à la seconde sur la demi-pointe	R – I – II
2–3			2 doubles ronds de jambe en l'air en dh 90°	
4	♩		R retiré	
	2 ♩		close R in V derrière on the whole foot	R – bras bas
1–16			repeat in reverse	

Adagio

32	3/4		V R devant	R – bras bas
1–2			pause	
1–2			R développé devant sur la demi-pointe	R – I – III
3			bend backwards	
4	♩		recover with R retiré	R – II
	2 ♩		close R in V devant on the whole foot	R – bras bas
1–2			L développé derrière sur la demi-pointe	R – I – II
3			penché	
4	♩		recover with L retiré	
	2 ♩		close L in V derrière on the whole foot	R – bras bas
1–2			R développé à la seconde sur la demi-pointe	R – I – II
3	♩		R retiré	
	2 ♩		close R in V devant sur la demi-pointe	
4	2 ♩		demi-détourné into V L devant	R on the barre, L – II
	♩		lower onto the whole foot	L – bras bas

1–2		L développé à la seconde sur la demi-pointe	L – I – II
3	♩	L retiré	
	2 ♩	close L in V devant sur la demi-pointe	
4	2 ♩	demi-détourné into V R devant	L on the barre, R – II
	♩	lower onto the whole foot	R – bras bas
1–2		R développé devant sur la demi-pointe	R – I – II
3		R tombé en avant, finishing L dégagé 90° derrière	R – III allongé
4		pause	
1		L through I into grand fouetté, finishing L derrière 90°	R on the barre, L – III allongé
2	2 ♩	pause	
	♩	R fondu	
3		L through I into grand fouetté, finishing L derrière 90°	L on the barre, R – III allongé
4	2 ♩	pause	
	♩	R fondu	
1–2		2 pirouettes en dd on R	arms – III
3		finishing L devant 90°	L on the barre, R – III
4		pause	
1		bend backwards	
2		recover	
3		close L in V devant on the whole foot	
4		L step en avant, finishing R pointe tendue derrière	R – III allongé

Battement double frappé

16	2/4	V R devant	R – bras bas
1	♩	relevé in V	R – I
	♩	R dégagé 45° à la seconde	R – II
1	♩	bt double frappé sur la demi-pointe, finishing pointe tendue croisé devant on the whole foot	R – bras bas – I – III
	♩	turning to the right (1/8) en face, L relevé with R à la seconde 45°	R – II
2	3 ♪	3 bts doubles frappés à la seconde sur la demi-pointe	
3	♩	bt double frappé sur la demi-pointe, finishing pointe tendue croisé derrière on the whole foot	R – bras bas – I – III
	♩	turning to the left en face, L relevé with R à la seconde 45°	R – II
4	3 ♪	3 bts double frappés à la seconde sur la demi-pointe	
1–2		petit bt sur le cou-de-pied (derrière–devant)	R – bras bas – I – II
3		L fondu with R sur le cou-de-pied devant temps relevé into 2 pirouettes en dh, finishing à la seconde sur la demi-pointe	R – I

4	3 ♪	bt battu effacé devant	R – I
	♪	turning to the left en face, R à la seconde 45°	R – II
1–8		repeat in reverse	

Grand battement

16	3/4	V R devant	R – bras bas
1–2		pause	R – I – II
1–2		2 grands bts devant	
3		3rd grand bt, finishing demi-rond de jambe en dh close R in V devant	
4		pause	
1–2		2 grands bts à la seconde	
3		3rd grand bt, finishing demi-rond de jambe en dh close R in V derrière	
4		pause	
1–4		4 grands bts en croix, close V R derrière	
1		grand bt derrière, finishing grand rond de jambe en dd close R in V devant	
2		pause	
3		grand bt devant, finishing grand rond de jambe en dh close R in V derrière	
4		pause	

The Exercises in the Centre

Petit adagio

32	3/4	V R croisé devant	arms – bras bas
1		pause	arms – I
2		V demi-plié	R – I, L – II
1–2		2 pirouettes en dh, finishing R croisé devant 90° en fondu	arms – I
3		R piqué en avant into attitude croisé derrière	L – III, R – II
4	2 ♩	close L in V derrière, turning to the right (1/8)	arms – II
	♩	en face V R devant in demi-plié	R – I, L – II
1–2		2 pirouettes en dh, finishing R à la seconde 90° en fondu	arms – I – II
3		R piqué de côté with L dégagé 90° à la seconde	
4		pause sur la demi-pointe	

| 1–2 | L demi-rond de jambe en dh, finishing attitude croisé derrière on the whole foot | L – III, R – II |
| 3–4 | renversé en dh, finishing wide IV L croisé devant (préparation for tours en dh) | arms – 3 arb |

Renversé en dehors.

1–2	2 tours en dh on R with L devant 90°, finishing facing 8 on the whole foot	R – III, L – II
3	L grand rond de jambe sur la demi-pointe, finishing 3rd arb to point 8 en fondu	arms – 3 arb
4	close L in V croisé derrière, straighten knees	arms – bras bas
1–16	repeat in reverse	

Renversé en dedans.

Battement tendu

16	2/4	V R croisé devant	arms – bras bas
1	♩	pause	arms – I
	♩	V demi-plié	R – I, L – II
1		2 pirouettes en dh on L, finishing R pointe tendue effacé devant	arms – I
2–3	4 ♩	R 4 bts tendus effacé devant	
4	3 ♪	R 3 bts jetés effacé devant, closing V R effacé devant in demi-plié	R – I, L – II
1		2 pirouettes en dd on R, finishing 1st arb à terre on R to point 2	arms – 1 arb
2–3	4 ♩	L 4 bts tendus effacé derrière	
4	3 ♪	L 3 bts jetés effacé derrière, closing V L derrière en face in demi-plié	R – I, L – II

1		2 pirouettes en dh on L, finishing en face R pointe tendue à la seconde	arms – I – II
2–3	4 ♩	R 4 bts tendus à la seconde, closing V devant, derrière . . .	
4	3 ♪	R 3 bts jetés à la seconde, closing V devant, derrière, devant . . .	
	♪	R dégagé 45° à la seconde	

1		flic-flac en tournant en dh into IV R croisé devant (préparation for pirouettes en dd)	R – I, L – II
2		2 pirouettes en dd on R into IV L croisé devant (préparation for pirouettes en dh)	arms – 3 arb
3		2 pirouettes en dh into V R croisé derrière in demi-plié	arms – I – bras bas
4		détourné into V R croisé devant	arms – I – III

Battement fondu

32	3/4	V R croisé devant	arms – bras bas
1–2			
1–2		R bt fondu croisé devant 45°	arms – I to L – III, R – II
3–4		L bt fondu croisé derrière 45°	arms – I – 3 arb
1		en face L fondu with R retiré devant	R – I, L – II
2		from grand temps relevé, tour en dh on L in attitude derrière, finishing facing 2	R – III, L – II
3–4		R bt fondu écarté derrière 90°	
1–8		repeat with other foot	
1–16		repeat in reverse	

Pirouettes

16	2/4	V R croisé devant	arms – bras bas
1	♩	en face L relevé with R sur le cou-de-pied devant	arms – I
	♩	close R in IV croisé derrière (préparation for pirouettes en dh)	arms – 3 arb
1		2 pirouettes en dh into IV R croisé derrière	arms – 3 arb
2		pause (préparation for pirouettes en dd)	L – I, R – II
3		2 pirouettes en dd into IV R croisé devant	arms – I – 3 arb
4		pause	
1		2 pirouettes en dh into IV L croisé derrière	arms – I – 3 arb
2		pause (préparation for pirouettes en dd)	R – I, L – II
3		2 pirouettes en dd into V L croisé devant in demi-plié	
4		en face straighten R with L dégagé à terre devant	L – I, R – II
1–2		chaînés to point 7, finishing en face, V L derrière in demi-plié	
	♩	relevé	R – I, L – II
3–4		chaînés to point 3, finishing en face, V R derrière in demi-plié	
		relevé	L – I, R – II
1–4		repeat the last 1–4 bars, finishing 2nd arb à terre on R to point 2	

Grand adagio

32	3/4	V R croisé devant	arms – bras bas
1		L step en avant to point 6 into 2nd arb à terre	
2		pause	
1		turning to the right, R piqué en avant to point 2 with L développé à la seconde, facing 4	arms – I to L – III, R – II
2		L tombé de côté to point 2, turning to the right facing 6, R through I into 2nd arb en fondu	arms – 2 arb
3		en face, pas de bourrée en dh, finishing R tombé en avant to point 2	arms – I R – I, L – II
4		2 tours en dd on R in attitude derrière, finishing facing 2 sur la demi-pointe	L – III, R – II
1–2		tour lent en dd sur la demi-pointe, finishing 3rd arb to point 8	
3–4		renversé en dh, finishing wide IV L croisé devant (préparation for tours en dd)	L – I, R – II
1–4		tour en dd on L in 1st arb, finishing facing 8 en fondu 1 pirouette en dd, finishing 1st arb facing 8 en fondu	
1–2		pas de bourrée en dh into V R croisé devant in demi-plié	arms – bras bas
3–4		L fondu with R dégagé à terre croisé devant demi-plié in IV transfer weight on R with L pointe tendue croisé derrière	arms – I L – III, R – II
1–4		6th port de bras, finishing wide IV R croisé devant (préparation for tours en dd)	R – I, L – II
1–2		2 tours en dd on R à la seconde, finishing en face	arms – III
3		L piqué de côté to point 7 with R dégagé 90° à la seconde	
4		pause	arms – II
1–4		R tombé de côté, renversé en dh, finishing V L croisé devant sur les demi-pointes	R – III, L – II arms – I – III
1–4		L tombé en avant to point 8 2 tours en dd on L in 1st arb, finishing facing 8 en fondu R soutenu en tournant en dd into V L croisé devant sur les demi-pointes	arms – III

Soutenu en tournant en dedans.

Grand battement

16	3/4	V L croisé devant	arms – bras bas
1–2		pause	
1–2		L step en avant to point 2	arms – I
		pas de ciseaux, finishing 1st arb on R	arms – III – 1 arb
3–4		pas de bourrée en dh into V L croisé devant	arms – bras bas
1–2		L 2 grands bts effacé devant	arms – I to R – III, L – II
3–4		R 2 grands bts effacé derrière, close V R croisé devant	arms – I – 1 arb
1–4		en face, 4 grands bts à la seconde (L, R, L, R), closing V devant	arms – I – II
1		L grand bt à la seconde, finishing demi-rond de jambe en dd close L in V croisé devant	R – III, L – II
2		pause	
3		en face, R grand bt à la seconde, finishing demi-rond de jambe en dd close R in V croisé devant	arms – II L – III, R – II
4		pause	

Allegro

The First Exercise

16	2/4	V L croisé devant	arms – bras bas
1	♩	en face, R glissade de côté to point 3, finishing V R devant	arms – II allongé – I
	♩	R jeté battu dessus	R – I, L – II
2	♩	L coupé dessous	
	♩	R ballonné dessous	L – I, R – II
3–4	3 ♩	3 assemblés battus dessus (R, L, R), close V R croisé devant	arms – bras bas
	♩	entrechat-quatre	
1–4		repeat with other foot	
1–8		repeat in reverse	

The Second Exercise

16	3/4	V R croisé devant	arms – bras bas
1		R sissonne tombé en tournant (to the right), finishing croisé en avant to point 8	arms – I to R – I, L – II
2		L assemblé derrière	arms – bras bas
3		R sissonne tombé en tournant (to the right), finishing de côté to point 3	arms – I – II
4		L assemblé dessus into V croisé devant	arms – bras bas
		R glissade de côté to point 3, finishing V L devant	arms – II allongé – I

1		R grand jeté de côté to point 3, finishing attitude croisé derrière on R, facing 8 (jeté passé)	L – III, R – II
2		L assemblé derrière	arms – bras bas
3–4		grande sissonne ouverte en tournant (to the left) into 3rd arb on L to point 2 en face R glissade de côté to point 3	arms – I – 3 arb
1–2		R cabriole fermée écarté devant, finishing V R devant L glissade de côté to point 7, finishing V R devant	R – I, L – II arms – II allongé – I
3–4		L cabriole fermée écarté devant, finishing V L devant R glissade de côté to point 3, finishing V R devant	L – I, R – II arms – II allongé – I
1–2		R grand jeté de côté to point 3, finishing L effacé devant (jeté passé)	R – III, L – II
3–4		L sissonne tombé effacé en avant, pas de bourrée, finishing 4th arb à terre on R to point 8	arms – I – 4 arb

The Third Exercise

16	3/4	V R croisé devant en diagonale from point 6 to point 2	arms – bras bas
1–2		R sissonne tombé effacé en avant, pas de bourrée, finishing R double rond de jambe en l'air en dh sauté, facing 8	arms – I to R – I, L – II arms – I to R – III, L – II
3–6		repeat twice	
7		R glissade sur les demi-pointes en avant to point 2, finishing V L croisé devant	arms – I to R – III, L – I arms – allongé
8		en face, L chassé de côté	arms – II allongé
1		saut de basque on R	arms – I – III
2		en face, L chassé de côté	arms – II allongé
3		saut de basque on R	arms – I – III
4		en face, L chassé de côté	arms – II allongé – I
5		saut de basque on R	arms – I – III
6		pause	arms – II
7–8		chaînés to point 8, finishing 2nd arb à terre on L	

The Fourth Exercise

16	3/4	1st arb à terre on R to point 2 en diagonale from point 6 to point 2	
1		pause	
2		facing 8, chassé de côté to point 6	arms – II allongé
1–2		jeté entrelacé, finishing 1st arb on R to point 2 facing 8 L chassé de côté to point 6	arms – I – 1 arb
3–6		repeat twice 1–2 bars	
7		L facing 8, L step de côté to point 6, with R pointe tendue croisé devant	R – I, L – II

Jeté entrelacé.

8		pause
1–6		6 grands jetés en tournant into 1st arb on R to point 2
7–8		chaînés, finishing 2nd arb à terre on R

The Fifth Exercise

16	3/4	V R croisé devant	arms – bras bas
1–4		R sissonne tombé effacé en avant, pas de bourrée	arms – I to R – III, L – I
		R wide glissade en avant to point 2	arms – II allongé – I
		grand jeté en avant in attitude effacé derrière onto R	L – III, R – II
1–4		repeat to the other side	
1–4		R sissonne tombé effacé en avant, pas de bourrée	arms – I to R – III, L – I
		R wide glissade en avant to point 2,	arms – II allongé – I
		into grand pas de chat,	R – III, L – I,
			arms – allongé
		finishing R glissade sur les demi-pointes en avant to point 2,	arms – I
		finishing V L croisé devant	L – I, R – II

Tour sissonne tombé.

1–2	2 times tour sissonne tombé to point 8
3–4	chaînés, finishing 2nd arb à terre on L

The Sixth Exercise

32	3/4	IV L pointe tendue croisé devant	arms – demi II
1		pause	
2		R wide glissade en avant to point 2	arms – II allongé – I
1–2		R grande cabriole effacé devant on L	L – III, R – II
		R step en avant to point 2	arms – I
3		L piqué en avant into 3rd arb	arms – 3 arb
4		L fondu with R sur le cou-de-pied derrière	R – I, L –II
1–2		R sissonne tombé croisé en arrière	
		L coupé dessous	arms – I

Sissonne tombé croisé en arrière.

Grand jeté en tournant in attitude croisé derrière.

		grand jeté en tournant in attitude croisé derrière onto R (grand jeté en tournant from croisé to croisé)	L – III, R – II
3		R relevé	
4		R fondu	arms – II
1–8		repeat to the other side	
1		en face, pas de bourrée suivi sur les demi-pointes de côté to point 7 in V L devant	arms – I
2		sissonne ouverte, finishing L petit développé à la seconde	L – III, R – I, arms – allongé
3–6		repeat 1–2 bars twice (to points 3 and 7)	
7		L assemblé dessous	arms – bras bas
8		relevé into V R croisé devant	R – I, L – II
1–4		4 times tour sissonne tombé to point 2	
1–4		chaînés, finishing 2nd arb à terre on R	

The Seventh Exercise

8	2/4	V L croisé devant	arms – bras bas
1	♩	en face R glissade de côté, finishing V L devant	arms – II allongé
	♩	R jeté battu dessus	R – I, L – II
2	♩	L coupé dessous	arms – I
	♩	R cabriole effacée devant on L	L – I, R – II
3	♩	turning to the right facing 4, R step en avant to point 6	arms – I
	♩	L ballonné battu dessous, finishing facing 8	R – I, L – II
4	♩	L coupé dessous	
	♩	R cabriole fermée croisé devant	arms – allongé
1–4		repeat to the other side	

The Exercises sur les Pointes

The First Exercise

8	2/4	V R croisé devant	arms – bras bas
1–2	4 ♩	4 échappés into II, changing position, turning to the right to points 3, 5, 7, 1,	arms – demi II allongé
		finishing V R devant	R – I, L – II
3	♩	1 pirouette en dh into V R croisé derrière	arms – I – bras bas
	♪	R relevé with L petit développé effacé devant	arms – I to L – I, R – II
	♪	L tombé en avant to point 8	
4	♩	L relevé into 1st arb	
	♪	close R in V croisé devant in demi-plié	arms – bras bas
	♪	détourné into V L croisé devant	
1–4		repeat to the other side	

The Second Exercise

16	3/4	V R croisé devant	arms – bras bas
1	2 ♩	en face, échappé into II	arms – I – II
	♩	demi-plié	
2	2 ♩	R relevé into 1 arb to point 2	
3		R relevé with L développé croisé devant	arms – I to R – III, L – II
		close L in V croisé devant in demi-plié	arms – II
4		relevé in V	arms – bras bas
1	2 ♩	en face, échappé into II	arms – I – II
	♩	demi-plié	
2	2 ♩	L relevé with R développé effacé devant	arms – I to L – III, R – II
3		L relevé with R développé in 3rd arb to point 2	arms – I – 3 arb
		close R in V croisé derrière in demi-plié	
4		relevé in V	arms – bras bas
1		en face, R relevé with L développé à la seconde	arms – I – II
2	2 ♩	fouetté-relevé (turning to the right), finishing L attitude effacé derrière	L – III, R – II
	♩	R fondu, with L petit développé croisé devant	arms – I
3–4		pas de bourrée suivi en avant to point 2, in V L croisé devant, finishing V L croisé devant	R – III, L – I, arms – allongé
	♩	L fondu with R sur le cou-de-pied derrière	L – I, R – II
1–2		pas de bourrée en tournant en dh, into IV R croisé devant (préparation for pirouette en dd)	R – I, L – II
3		2 pirouettes en dd into V L croisé devant in demi-plié	arms – I – III
4		relevé in V	

The Third Exercise

16	3/4	2 arb à terre on R to point 2	
1		balancé on L, turning to the left facing 8	R – I, L – II
2		R piqué en avant to point 2 into 1st arb	arms – 1 arb
3		balancé on L, turning to the left facing 8	R – I, L – II
4		R piqué en avant to point 2 with L développé croisé devant	arms – I to R – III, L – II
1		close L in V croisé devant sur les pointes	arms – III
2		détourné into V R croisé devant	
3		L holding sur la pointe, with R petit développé croisé avant	
4		R tombé en avant to point 8 into wide IV (préparation for tours en dd)	arms – II R – I, L – II
1		tour en dd in 1st arb on R, finishing facing 2 en fondu	
2		repeat tour	
3–4		pas de bourrée en dh into wide IV L croisé devant (préparation for tours en dd)	arms – I to L – I, R – II
1		tour en dd à la seconde on L,	arms – III
2		finishing en face en fondu	arms – II
3		R soutenu en tournant en dd into V L croisé devant	arms – I – III
4		L step en avant to point 8 into 2nd arb à terre	

The Fourth Exercise

16	3/4		V R croisé devant	arms – bras bas
1	2 ♩		en face, L relevé with R développé à la seconde	arms – I – II
	♩		L fondu	
2	2 ♩		L relevé with R double rond de jambe en l'air en dh 90°, finishing effacé devant	R – III, L – II
	♩		R tombé en avant to point 2 into 1st arb	
3–4			pas de bourrée en dh into V L croisé devant in demi-plié	arms – bras bas
1–4			repeat 1–4 bars to the other side	
1			L relevé with R développé à la seconde	arms – I – II
2			grand fouetté en tournant en dd, finishing 3rd arb on L fondu to point 2	arms – 3 arb
3			L relevé in attitude croisé derrière	R – III, L – II
4			close R in wide IV croisé derrière with L fondu (préparation for tours en dh)	arms – 3 arb
1			tour en dh in attitude derrière on L,	arms – III
2			finishing point 2 en fondu	arms – II
3			pas de bourrée en tournant en dh into V R croisé devant in demi-plié	arms – bras bas
4			L glissade sur les pointes en avant to point 8, finishing V R croisé devant	L – III, R – II, arms – allongé
1–16			repeat the whole exercise in reverse	

The Fifth Exercise

8	2/4	IV R pointe tendue croisé devant en diagonale from point 6 to point 2	R – I, L – II
1–2	3 ♩	3 times pirouette-piqué en dd on R	
	♪	R glissade sur les pointes en tournant into V R effacé devant	
	♪	demi-plié	
3–4	3 ♩	3 times pirouette en dh on L, finishing point 2, into V R effacé devant	
	2 ♪	2 chaînés to point 2	
1–4		repeat the whole exercise, close 2nd arb à terre on R to point 2	

The Sixth Exercise

8	2/4	V R croisé devant	arms – bras bas
1	♩	pause	
	♩	L fondu with R petit développé effacé devant	arms – I
1	♩	R tombé–relevé en avant to point 2 into 2nd arb 45°	arms – 2 arb
	♩	R relevé with L petit développé effacé devant	L – III, R – II
2	♩	L tombé–relevé en avant to point 8 into 2nd arb 45°	arms – 2 arb
	♪	L relevé with R petit développé effacé devant	R – III, L – II
	♪	L fondu	
3	♪	R piqué en avant to point 2 into attitude effacé derrière	L – III, R – II
	3 ♪	3 temps levés sur la pointe on R, turning to the right, finishing facing 2	
4	♪	R fondu	
	♪	R relevé into attitude effacé derrière	
	♪	close L in V croisé devant in demi-plié	arms – I – demi II allongé
	♪	relevé in V	
1–4		repeat to the other side	

The Seventh Exercise

8	2/4	IV L devant en face 7 (préparation for pirouettes en dh)	arms – 3 arb
1–8	16 ♩	16 tours fouettés, finishing IV R croisé derrière	arms – II

The Eighth Exercise

8	2/4	IV R pointe tendue devant en face in a circle from point 8	R – I, L – II
1–7	14 ♩	14 pirouettes-piqués en dd on R	
8		chaînés, finishing 2nd arb à terre on R to point 2	

LESSON TWO

The Exercises at the Barre

Plié

64	3/4	I position	R – bras bas
1–2		pause	R – I – II
1–4		I position, grand plié	R – bras bas – I – II
1–3		grand plié	R – bras bas – I – III – II
4		relevé	
1–7		3 ports de bras sur les demi-pointes	
8		L on the whole foot, R dégagé à terre à la seconde	R – II
1–4		II position, grand plié	R – bras bas – I – II
1–4		grand plié, finishing R pointe tendue à la seconde	R – bras bas – I – III – II
1–4		bend sideways to the right	R – III
1–3		recover	R – II
4		close R in V devant	
1–4		V position, grand plié	R – bras bas – I – II
1–4		grand plié	R – bras bas – I – III – II
1–2		demi-plié, 1 pirouette en dh	
3–4		pause (R retiré, L sur la demi-pointe)	
1–2		bend backwards	
3		recover	
4		1/2 pirouette en dd (to the left), close R in V derrière on the whole foot	R on the barre, L – I – II
1–4		V position, grand plié	L – bras bas – I – II
1–4		grand plié	L – bras bas – I – III – II
1–2		demi-plié, 1 pirouette en dh	
3–4		pause (L retiré, R sur la demi-pointe)	
1–2		bend backwards	
3		recover	
4		1/2 pirouette en dd (to the right), close L in V derrière on the whole foot	L on the barre, R – I – II

Battement tendu

16	2/4		V R devant	R – bras bas
1				
1–3	6 ♩		R 6 bts tendus devant, closing in demi-plié	R – I – III
4	♩		R glissade en avant	
	♩		L dégagé à terre derrière, straighten R	R – 2 arb
1–3	6 ♩		L 6 bts tendus derrière, closing in demi-plié	
4	♩		L glissade en arrière	
	♩		R dégagé à terre à la seconde, straighten L	R – II

1–3	6 ♩	R 6 bts tendus à la seconde, closing V derrière, devant . . . close V R devant in demi-plié	
4	♩	R glissade de côté, finishing V R devant	L – I, R – II
	♩	L dégagé à terre à la seconde, straighten L	
1–3	6 ♩	L 6 bts tendus à la seconde, closing V devant, derrière . . . close V L derrière in demi-plié	
4	♩	L glissade de côté, finishing V R devant	L on the barre, R – I
	♩	straighten knees	R – II

Battement jeté

16	2/4		
1	3 ♪	R 3 bts jetés devant	
	♪	R dégagé 45° devant	
2		R 2 bts jetés balançoires, closing V R devant	
3	3 ♪	L 3 bts jetés derrière	
	♪	L dégagé 45° derrière	
4		L 2 bts jetés balançoires, closing V L derrière	
1	3 ♪	R 3 bts jetés devant	R – III
2	3 ♪	R 3 bts jetés à la seconde, closing V derrière, devant, derrière . . .	R – I – II
	♪	R dégagé 45° derrière	
3–4		R 6 bts jetés balançoires, closing V R derrière	
1–6		repeat 1–6 bars in reverse	
7–8		R 8 bts jetés à la seconde, each closing I, and concluding V devant	R – bras bas – I – II

Rond de jambe à terre

48	3/4	I position	R – bras bas
1–2		préparation en dh	R – I – II
1–2		2 ronds à terre	
3–4		rond à terre, finishing grand bt devant, passé développé derrière	R – I – III – II
1		3 ronds à terre	
2–3		2 grands ronds de jambe jetés,	
4	·	finishing pointe tendue devant	
1–8		repeat 1–8 bars	
1–16		repeat the whole exercise in reverse, close V L devant	R – bras bas
1		L développé devant	R – I – II
2		pause	
3–4		R fondu with bend forwards	R – I
1		R straighten, with recover	R – III
2		bend backwards	
3		recover	R – II
4		close L in V devant	R – bras bas

1		R développé derrière	R – I – II
2		pause	
3		L deepen fondu with R pointe tendue derrière	R – 2 arb
4		pause	
1		L holding fondu, rising a little with R dégagé 90° derrière	
2		L relevé in attitude derrière	R – III
3		R retiré	
4		close R in V derrière	R – II – bras bas

Battement fondu

16	3/4	V R devant	R – bras bas
1–2			
1–2		R bt fondu devant	R – I – II
3		demi-rond de jambe en dh, finishing en fondu	
4		tour fouetté en dh, finishing R à la seconde sur la demi-pointe	
1–2		R bt fondu effacé devant 90°	R – bras bas – I – III
3–4		turning to the left, R bt fondu effacé derrière 90°	R – I – 2 arb
1–8		repeat in reverse, finishing R à la seconde 45° sur la demi-pointe	R – II

Battement frappé

8	2/4		
1	2 ♩	R 2 bts frappés devant	R – I – III
2	3 ♪	3 bts frappés devant	
3–4	7 ♪	7 bts frappés à la seconde	R – I – II
1–4		repeat in reverse	

Rond de jambe en l'air

16	2/4	V R devant	R – bras bas
1		préparation – temps relevé en dh	R – I – II
1	3 ♪	3 ronds en l'air en dh, finishing en fondu	
2	♩	double rond de jambe en l'air en dh sauté	
	♩	L relevé with R double rond de jambe en l'air en dh	
3–4		repeat 1–2 bars	
1–2	3 ♩	3 doubles ronds de jambe en l'air (en dh, en dd, en dh)	
	♩	pause	
3		L fondu with R sur le cou-de-pied devant from temps relevé 2 pirouettes en dh, finishing écarté derrière 90°	R – I R – III
4	♩	double rond de jambe en l'air en dh 90°	
	♪	close R in V derrière sur les demi-pointes	
	♪	détourné into V R devant, finishing R dégagé 45° à la seconde	
1–8		repeat the whole exercise in reverse	

Adagio

32	3/4	V R devant	R – bras bas
1–2			
1		R développé effacé devant sur la demi-pointe	R – I – III
2		pause	
3		L fondu	
4		L relevé with R demi-rond de jambe en dh, finishing écarté derrière	
1		fouetté (turning to the left), finishing R effacé derrière	
2		pause	
3–4		R demi-rond de jambe en dd, finishing en fondu	R – I – II
1–2		2 pirouettes en dd, finishing R attitude devant	R – III
3–4		L fondu with bend forwards	R – I
1–3		L relevé with R grand rond de jambe	R – II – 2 arb
4		close R in V derrière on the whole foot	R – bras bas
1–16		repeat in reverse	

Battement double frappé

16	2/4	V R devant	R – bras bas
1	♩	relevé in V	R – I
	♩	R dégagé 45° à la seconde	R – II
1	♩	bt double frappé sur la demi-pointe, finishing pointe tendue devant	R – I – III
	♩	repeat the same derrière	R – 2 arb
2	3 ♪	3 bts doubles frappés à la seconde sur la demi-pointe	
3	♩	bt double frappé sur la demi-pointe, finishing pointe tendue derrière	R – 2 arb
	♩	repeat the same devant	R – III
4	3 ♪	3 bts doubles frappés à la seconde sur la demi-pointe	R – I – II
1–2		R petit bt sur le cou-de-pied (derrière–devant)	R – bras bas – I – II
3		L fondu with R sur le cou-de-pied devant from temps relevé 2 pirouettes en dh, finishing R à la seconde 45°	R – I — R – II
4		R bt battu effacé devant, turning to the left en face, R à la seconde 45°	
1–8		repeat in reverse	

Grand battement

16	3/4	V R devant	R – bras bas
1–2		pause	R – I – II
1–3		3 grands bts devant	
4		pause	
1–3		3 grands bts à la seconde, closing V derrière, devant, derrière . . .	
4		pause	

1–2	2 grands bts derrière	
3	3rd grand bt through I into dégagé à terre devant	R – bras bas – I
4	pause	
1–3	3 times posé pirouette-piqué en dh on L, finishing R écarté derrière (every time)	L on the barre, R – III
4	close R in V derrière on the whole foot	

The Exercises in the Centre

Petit adagio

16	3/4	V R croisé devant	arms – bras bas
1–2			
1	2 ♩	en face R développé à la seconde	arms – I – II
	♩	L relevé with R écarté devant	
2		grand fouetté en tournant en dd, finishing 1st arb to point 8 en L fondu	

Grand fouetté en tournant en dedans.

3–4	1 pirouette en dd on L, finishing 1st arb to point 8 en fondu	arms – I – 1 arb
1–2	pas de bourrée en dh into wide IV R croisé devant (préparation for tours en dh)	arms – I – 3 arb
3–4	2 tours en dh on R in attitude derrière, finishing facing 8 en fondu	
1	1 pirouette en dh, finishing face L à la seconde 90°	
2	pause	
3–4	L tombé de côté, renversé en dh, finishing wide IV R croisé devant (préparation for tours en dd)	R – I, L – II

Tombé de côté, renversé en dehors.

1–2	2 tours en dd on R in attitude derrière, finishing facing 2 en fondu	L – III, R – II arms – allongé
3–4	L soutenu en tournant en dd into V R croisé devant	arms – I – III

Battement tendu

16	2/4	V R croisé devant	
1			
1	2 ♩	R 2 bts tendus croisé devant	L – III, R – II
		closing in demi-plié	R – I, L – II
2		2 pirouettes en dh into V R croisé derrière	arms – I – bras bas
3–4	4 ♩	R 4 bts tendus croisé derrière	arms – I – 3 arb
1	2 ♩	L 2 bts tendus croisé devant,	R – III, L – II
		closing in demi-plié	L – I, R – II
2		2 pirouettes en dh into V L croisé derrière	arms – I – bras bas
3–4	4 ♩	L 4 bts tendus croisé derrière	arms – I – 3 arb
1	2 ♩	en face, R 2 bts tendus à la seconde, closing V derrière, devant	arms – II
2	3 ♪	R 3 bts jetés à la seconde, closing V derrière, devant, derrière	
3	2 ♩	L 2 bts tendus à la seconde, closing V derrière, devant	
4	3 ♪	L 3 bts jetés à la seconde, closing V derrière, devant, derrière	
		close V L derrière in demi-plié	
1	♩	R assemblé dessus	R – I, L – II
	♩	2 pirouettes en dh into IV R croisé derrière	arms – I – 3 arb
2		pause (préparation for pirouettes en dd)	L – I, R – II
3		2 pirouettes en dd into V R croisé devant in demi-plié	
4		détourné into V L croisé devant	arms – I – III

Battement fondu

16	3/4	V R croisé devant	arms – bras bas
1–2		pause	
1–2		en face, R bt fondu à la seconde 90°	arms – I – II
3		L fondu	
4	2 ♩	fouetté relevé, finishing 1st arb to point 7	arms – 1 arb
	♩	close R in V croisé devant sur les demi-pointes	arms – bras bas
1–2		en face L bt fondu à la seconde 90°	arms – I – II
3		R fondu	
4	2 ♩	fouetté relevé, finishing L effacé devant	R – III, L – II
	♩	close L in V croisé derrière sur les demi-pointes	arms – bras bas
1–2		facing 2, R bt fondu écarté derrière	arms I to R – III, L – II
3		fouetté, finishing 1st arb to point 8	
4		pas de bourrée en dh into V R croisé devant sur les demi-pointes	arms – I – III
1		R tombé en avant to point 2, tour en dd in 1st arb, finishing facing 2, on R fondu	
2		repeat tour	
3		1 pirouette en dd on R, finishing 1st arb to point 2 en fondu	arms – 1 arb
4		pas de bourrée en dh into V L croisé devant	arms – bras bas

Pirouettes

8		IV R pointe tendue croisé devant en diagonale from point 6 to point 2	R – I, L – II
1–2	3 ♩	3 times pirouette-piqué en dd on R	
	♩	2 pirouettes-piqués en dd on R	
3–4	3 ♩	3 times posé pirouette-piqué en dh on L	
	♩	2 times pirouette-piqué en dh on L	
1–2	3 ♩	3 times pirouette-piqué en dd on R	
		2 pirouettes-piqués en dd on R, finishing L coupé dessous with R sur le cou-de-pied devant	
3–4		chaînés, finishing 2nd arb à terre on R	

Grand adagio

32	3/4	V R croisé devant	arms – bras bas
1		pause	
2		demi-plié-relevé-demi-plié	arms – demi II allongé
1		entrechat-six into IV L croisé devant (préparation for pirouettes en dh)	arms – I – III – 3 arb
2		pause	
3		2 pirouettes en dh on L, finishing R attitude croisé derrière	arms – I to R – III, L – II
4		pause	
1–2	♩	L fondu with bend sideways to the right tour lent en dh, finishing facing 2, bend backwards	L – III, R – II arms – II
3–4		pas de bourrée en tournant en dh into wide IV R croisé devant (préparation for tours en dd)	arms – I to R – I, L – II
1–2		2 tours en dd on R in 1st arb, finishing facing 2	
3–4		tour lent en dd, finishing 3rd arb to point 8 en L fondu	
1		facing 8, grand jeté en arrière to point 4 on L, finishing R croisé devant	L – III, R – II
2		L relevé	
3		R tombé en avant to point 8 into wide IV (préparation for tours en dd)	R – I, L – II
4		pause	
1–2		2 tours en dd on R à la seconde, finishing en face en fondu	arms – III
3		en face L piqué de côté with R dégagé 90° à la seconde	arms – II
4		pause	
1–4		R tombé de côté, renversé en dh, finishing V L croisé devant sur les demi-pointes	arms – bras bas
1–2		en face L développé à la seconde	arms – I – II
3		close L in demi-plié II	L – I, R – II
4		1 tour en dh on R à la seconde, finishing en face en fondu	arms – III
1–2		1 pirouette en dh into IV L croisé derrière	arms – I – 3 arb
3–4		2 pirouettes en dh into IV L croisé derrière	arms – III to R – III, L – II

Grand battement

16	3/4	IV R pointe tendue croisé devant	R – I, L – II
1–2			
1–4		4 times posé pirouette-piqué en dh on L to point 2, finishing R développé écarté devant (every time)	arms – I to R – III, L – II
1		R tombé en avant to point 2 into 1st arb	arms – I – 1 arb
2		pas de bourrée en dh into IV L croisé devant (préparation for pirouette en dh)	arms – I – 3 arb
3–4		2 pirouettes en dh into V R croisé derrière	arms – I – bras bas
1		L grand bt croisé devant	arms – I to R – III, L – II
2		R grand bt croisé derrière	arms – I – 3 arb
3–4		repeat 1–2 bars grands bts L, R	
1–2		en face 2 grands bts à la seconde (R, L), closing V devant	arms – I – II
3–4		2 grands bts à la seconde, through retiré (R, L) into V devant	arms – bras bas

Allegro

The First Exercise

16	2/4		V R croisé devant	arms – bras bas
1	♩		entrechat-cinq on R with L sur le cou-de-pied derrière, facing 8	arms – I to L – I, R – II
	♪		L coupé dessous	arms – I
	♪		R assemblé croisé devant	arms – bras bas
2	♩		entrechat-trois on R with L sur le cou-de-pied devant, facing 2	arms – I to R – I, L – II
	♪		L coupé dessus	arms – I
	♪		R assemblé croisé derrière	arms – bras bas
3–4			repeat 1–2 bars with other foot	
1–2	3 ♩		en face 3 assemblés battus dessus (L, R, L)	
	♩		straighten knees	
3–4	3 ♩		3 assemblés battus dessous (L, R, L)	
	♩		royale	
1–8			repeat the whole exercise	

The Second Exercise

16	3/4	V R croisé devant	arms – bras bas
1		sissonne ouverte en tournant en dh (to the right), finishing R petit développé à la seconde	arms – I – II
2		R double rond de jambe en l'air en dh sauté	
3		L relevé with R double rond de jambe en l'air en dh	
4		close R in V croisé derrière in demi-plié	
1–4		repeat with other foot, close V R croisé devant	

1		grande sissonne ouverte battu en avant to point 8, into 3rd arb on R	arms – I – 3 arb
2		L assemblé croisé derrière	arms – bras bas
3		royale	arms – I – II
4		straighten knees	arms – bras bas
1		facing 8, grande sissonne ouverte battu en arrière to point 6 on R, finishing L croisé devant	arms – I to R – III, L – II
2		L assemblé croisé devant	arms – bras bas
3		entrechat-quatre	arms – I – II
4		straighten knees	arms – bras bas

The Third Exercise

16	3/4*	V L croisé devant	arms – bras bas
1	♩	en face, R grand jeté de côté to point 3, finishing L passé développé effacé devant (jeté passé)	arms – I R – III, L – II
	2 ♩	2 steps en avant to point 8 (L, R)	arms – II
2		en face, L grand jeté de côté to point 7, finishing R passé développé effacé devant	arms – I L – III, R – II
		2 steps en avant to point 2 (R, L)	arms – II
3		repeat 1st bar	
4		en face, L glissade sur les demi-pointes, finishing V L croisé devant	R – I, L – II
1		grand jeté en avant to point 3 in 2nd arb on R	arms – I – 2 arb
		en face, L glissade de côté, finishing V R devant	arms – I
2		repeat grand jeté and glissade to the other side	
3		2 pirouettes-piqués en dd on R to point 4, into V L croisé derrière in demi-plié	arms – III
4		relevé in V	
1–2	♩	L ballonné effacé devant	L – I, R – II
	2 ♩	L tombé en avant to point 8, R coupé dessous	arms – I
	♩	grand pas de basque, finishing on L with R croisé devant	arms – III – I
	♩	R tombé dessus with L sur le cou-de-pied derrière	R – I, L – II
	♩	L coupé dessous	
3–6		repeat ballonné and grand pas de basque to points 2, 8	
7		2 pirouettes-piqués en dd on R to point 2, finishing 1st arb à terre on R to point 2	
8		pause	

The Fourth Exercise

16	3/4	IV R pointe tendue croisé devant en diagonale from point 6 to point 2	R – I, L – II
1		pause	
2		facing 8, R chassé de côté to point 2	arms – II allongé
1–4		saut de basque on L	arms – III
		R chassé de côté to point 2	arms – II allongé
		saut de basque on L	arms – III

*mazurka

1–2		chaînés	
3		R glissade sur les demi-pointes en tournant en dd, finishing V R croisé devant	arms – I – III
4		pause	

1–2		pas couru en avant to point 8	arms – bras bas – II allongé
		pas de poisson, finishing L attitude croisé derrière on R	L – III, R – II, arms – allongé
3–4		repeat pas couru and pas de poisson	

1–4		L glissade de côté, finishing V R devant	arms – I
		L grand jeté de côté, finishing renversé en dh	L – III, R – II
		L glissade sur les demi-pointes en avant to point 8, finishing V R croisé devant	arms – I – 1 arb

The Fifth Exercise

8	2/4	V L croisé devant	arms – bras bas

1		facing 2, R sissonne tombé croisé derrière	arms – I to R – I, L – II
		L coupé dessous	arms – I
	♩	grand jeté en tournant in attitude croisé derrière on R facing 8,	L – III, R – II
2	♩	L assemblé croisé derrière	arms – bras bas
	♩	entrechat-quatre	
3–4		repeat with other foot to the other side	

1	♩	L sissonne tombé effacé en avant	arms – I to L – I, R – II
		R coupé dessous	arms – I
	♩	grand jeté en tournant in attitude effacé derrière on L facing 8, R coupé dessous	R – III, L – II
2		repeat sissonne tombé effacé en avant and grand jeté	
3	2 ♩	2 times tour sissonne tombé to point 8	
4		chaînés to point 8, finishing 2nd arb à terre on L	

The Sixth Exercise

16	3/4	IV L pointe tendue croisé devant	arms – demi II

1			
2		pas de bourrée en avant to point 2	arms – demi II allongé – I

1–2		grand jeté en avant in attitude croisé derrière on L	R – III, L – II
		pas de bourrée en avant to point 2	arms – demi II allongé
3–4		repeat grand jeté en avant	

1–2		R sissonne tombé effacé en avant	arms – I to R – III, L – II
		pas de bourrée	arms – I
3		R sissonne temps levé in 1st arb to point 3	
4		en face, L glissade de côté to point 7	arms – II allongé

1		L sissonne temps levé in 1st arb to point 7, finishing failli en avant	R – I, L – II
2		R sissonne temps levé in 4th arb to point 7	arms – 4 arb

3–4		L wide glissade en avant to point 8	arms – I
		grand jeté en avant in 1st arb to point 8 on L	
		en face, R glissade de côté to point 3	arms – II allongé
1		R sissonne temps levé in 1st arb to point 3,	
		finishing failli en avant	
2		L sissonne temps levé in 4th arb to point 3	
3–4		R wide glissade en avant to point 2	
		grand jeté en avant in 1st arb to point 2 on R	
		R relevé in 1st arb	

The Seventh Exercise

16	3/4	IV L pointe tendue croisé devant	arms – demi II
		en diagonale from point 6 to point 2	
1		pause	
2		R wide glissade en avant	arms – I
1–2		grand pas de chat	R – III, L – I,
			arms – allongé
		R wide glissade en avant	
3–4		repeat 1–2 bars	
1–4		grand jeté en avant into 1st arb on R	
		R relevé	
		facing 8, L chassé de côté to point 6	arms – II allongé
1–2		jeté entrelacé, finishing 1st arb to point 2 on R	arms – I – III – 1 arb
		facing 8, L chassé de côté to point 6	arms – II allongé
3–4		repeat jeté entrelacé and chassé	
1–2		R grand assemblé dessus en tournant en dd,	arms – I – III
		finishing V R croisé devant	R – I, L – II
3–4		2 pirouettes en dh on L into IV R croisé derrière	arms – II

The Eighth Exercise

8	2/4	V R croisé devant	arms – bras bas
1	2 ♩	brisé dessus-dessous to point 8	
2	♩	L ballonné battu en avant, finishing L sur le cou-de-pied	R – I, L – II
		derrière	
	♩	pas de bourrée en tournant en dh into V L croisé devant	arms – bras bas
3–4		repeat to the other side	
1	4 ♪	4 emboîtés en tournant en dd to point 2 (on R, L, R, L) (sur le	
		cou-de-pied devant)	
2	♩	1 pirouette en dh on L into V R effacé devant, facing 2	
	♩	1 pirouette en dh on L, finishing facing 8, L fondu with R sur	
		le cou-de-pied devant	R – I, L – II
3–4		chaînés to point 2, finishing 2nd arb à terre on R	

The Exercises sur les Pointes

The First Exercise

8	2/4	V R croisé devant	arms – bras bas
1	♩	en face, échappé into II*,	arms – I – II
	♪	finishing demi-plié in II	arms – I
	♪	R relevé with L développé croisé devant	R – III, L – II
2	2 ♪	L tombé en avant to point 2, relevé into 3rd arb	
	♩	L fondu, 1 pirouette en dh, finishing facing 8	
3	♪	close R in V croisé devant in demi-plié	arms – bras bas
	♪	échappé into IV R croisé devant	arms – 4 arb
	♪	holding sur les pointes into IV, turning to the right, finishing facing 4, IV L devant	
	♪	pause	
4	♪	V L devant in demi-plié	arms – bras bas
	♩	échappé into II, turning to the right en face, finishing V R croisé devant in demi-plié	arms – I – II arms – bras bas
	♪	en face, échappé into II,	
1–4	♪	finishing V L croisé devant in demi-plié repeat to the other side	arms – bras bas

The Second Exercise

16	3/4	IV L pointe tendue croisé devant	arms – demi II
1	2 ♩		
	♩	L fondu	
1	♩	en face, L relevé with R dégagé 90° à la seconde	arms – I to R – III, L – II, arms – allongé
	♩	L holding sur la pointe, R retiré	
	♩	R tombé dessus with L pointe tendue derrière, knee bent	R – II – I, L – II, arms – allongé
2–3		repeat 1st bar (L, R), finishing R fondu with L sur le cou-de-pied derrière	
4		pas de bourrée en dh into V L croisé devant	arms – bras bas
1		L glissé en avant to point 7, relevé into 1st arb	arms – I – 1 arb
2		L relevé with R sur le cou-de-pied devant, turning to the right facing 2	arms – I with wrists crossed on the chest
3		R glissé en avant to point 3, relevé into 1st arb	arms – I – 1 arb
4		R relevé with L sur le cou-de-pied devant, turning to the left facing 8	arms – I with wrists crossed on the chest
1–2		en face, L tombé de côté and renversé en dh, finishing facing 2, R fondu with L petit développé écarté devant	arms – I – demi II allongé
3–4		pas de bourrée suivi de côté to point 4 in V L devant	R – III, L – I, arms – allongé

*Begin échappé into the first quarter of the first bar

1–2		en face, R tombé de côté and renversé en dh, finishing facing 8, L fondu with R petit développé écarté devant	arms – I – demi II allongé
3–4		pas de bourrée suivi de côté to point 6 in V R devant,	L – III, R – I, arms – allongé
	♩	finishing V R croisé devant sur les pointes	arms – III

The Third Exercise

16	3/4	2 arb à terre on R to point 2	arms – 2 arb
1		facing 2, L piqué en arrière to point 6 with R dégagé 90° effacé devant	L – III, R – II
2		L fondu with bend backwards	
3		recover, R piqué en avant to point 2 into 1st arb	arms – I – 1 arb
4		R fondu with penché into 1st arb	
1		L piqué en arrière to point 6 with R dégagé 90° effacé devant	L – III, R – II
2		L fondu	
3		fouetté relevé (to the left), finishing 1st arb to point 6 on L fondu	arms – 1 arb
4	♩	facing 6, close R V devant in demi-plié	arms – bras bas
	♩	R relevé with L développé 1st arb to point 6	arms – I – 1 arb
	♩	R fondu	
1		L through I into grand fouetté (to the right), finishing 1st arb to point 2 on R	arms – I – III – 1 arb
2		R fondu	
3–4		pas de bourrée en dh into IV L croisé devant (préparation for pirouettes en dh)	arms – I – 3 arb
1		2 pirouettes en dh into IV R croisé derrière	arms – I – 3 arb
2	2 ♩	pause	
	♩	R coupé dessous	
3		L step en avant to point 8 into 2nd arb à terre	arms – I – 2 arb
4		pause	

The Fourth Exercise

16	2/4	V R croisé devant	arms – bras bas
1	♩	facing 8, L glissade sur les pointes en avant to point 8, finishing IV R croisé devant	arms – I – III
	♩	R fondu with L pointe tendue effacé devant	R – I, L – II
2		R relevé with L through I into attitude croisé derrière	L – III, R – II
		pas de bourrée en tournant en dh into V L croisé devant	arms – I – bras bas
3–4		repeat to the other side, finishing V R croisé devant	
1–2	♪	facing 8, L piqué de côté to point 6 with R double bt frappé écarté devant	R – I, L – II
	♪	R tombé dessus with L sur le cou-de-pied derrière	
	2 ♩	repeat 2 times piqué with tombé	
	♪	L piqué de côté to point 6 with R développé croisé devant	arms – I to L – III, R – II
	♪	L fondu	

3–4		facing 8, pas de bourrée suivi en avant to point 8 in V R croisé devant, finishing point 7	L – III, R – I, arms – allongé
	♩	en face, R glissade de côté, finishing V L devant	arms – I
1		R piqué en avant to point 3 into 1st arb	arms – 1 arb
		R holding sur la pointe, L retiré, turning to the left en face L coupé dessous	R – III, L – I
		R glissade de côté, finishing V L devant	arms – I
2		repeat piqué and glissade,	
3	♩	R piqué en avant to point 3 into 1st arb	
	♩	close L in V croisé devant in demi-plié	arms – bras bas
4	♩	détourné into V R croisé devant	arms – I – III
	♩	facing 8, L step de côté to point 6, finishing R pointe tendue croisé devant	R – I, L – II
1	♩	posé pirouette-piqué en dh on L to point 2	
	♩	posé pirouette-piqué en dh on L, finishing R développé écarté devant	R – III, L – II
2		repeat 1st bar with pirouettes	
3–4	♩	posé pirouette–piqué en dh on L	
	3 ♩	chaînés, finishing 1st arb à terre to point 2 on R	

The Fifth Exercise

8	2/4	V R croisé devant	arms – bras bas
1	♩	facing 8, sissonne simple devant on L into V R croisé devant	arms – I to R – I, L – II
	♩	L relevé with R double rond de jambe en l'air en dh, finishing V R croisé derrière, facing 2	arms – bras bas
2		repeat to the other side	
3–4	4 ♩	4 sissonnes simples devant (on L, R, L, R), into V derrière, changing épaulement, finishing V R croisé devant	
1	♩	entrechat-quatre	
	♩	1 pirouette en dh on L into V R croisé derrière	
2		repeat entrechat-quatre and pirouette with other foot	
3	2 ♩	en face repeat twice pirouette en dh on L, finishing V devant	
4	♩	2 pirouettes en dh on L into V R croisé derrière	arms – bras bas
	♩	relevé in V	arms – I – III

The Sixth Exercise

8	2/4	V R croisé devant	arms – bras bas
1	♩		
	♩	relevé in V	arms – demi II allongé
1–2	6 ♪	facing 8, R 6 ballonnés sautés sur la pointe écarté devant travelling de côté to point 2	R – I, L – II, arms – allongé
	♪	L holding sur la pointe, straighten knee with R double rond de jambe en l'air en dh	
	♪	R tombé dessus sur la pointe with L sur le cou-de-pied derrière	arms – bras bas – I
3–4	♪	R temps levé sur la pointe	

	3 ♪	R 3 temps levés sur la pointe with L attitude croisé derrière	L – III, R – II
	♪	R fondu on the whole foot	
	3 ♪	pas de bourrée en tournant en dh into V L croisé devant sur les pointes	arms – bras bas – I – demi II allongé
1–4		repeat to the other side	

The Seventh Exercise

4	2/4	IV R pointe tendue croisé devant en diagonale from point 6 to point 2	R – I, L – II
1	♩	pirouette-piqué en dd on R	
	2 ♪	2 chaînés	
2–4		repeat 3 times, finishing 2nd arb à terre on R	

The Eighth Exercise

12	2/4	IV L devant en face (préparation for pirouettes en dh)	arms – 3 arb
1–12		24 tours fouettés, finishing IV R croisé derrière	arms – II

The Ninth Exercise

8	2/4	IV R pointe tendue devant en face in a circle from point 8	R – I, L – II
1–8	16 ♩	16 pirouettes-piqués en dd on R, finishing 1st arb à terre on R to point 2	

LESSON THREE

The Exercises at the Barre

Plié

88	3/4	I position	R – bras bas
1–2		pause	R – I – II
1–4		I position, grand plié	R – bras bas – I – II
1–4		grand plié	R – III – I – II
1–2		demi-plié, 1 pirouette en dh	R – I – II
3–4		pause (R retiré, L sur la demi-pointe)	
1–2		R petit développé à la seconde	
3–4		L on the whole foot, R pointe tendue à la seconde	
1–4		II position, demi-plié	R – bras bas – I – II
1–4		grand plié	R – bras bas – I – II
1–4		grand plié	R – III – I – II
1		relevé	arms – II
2		pause sur les demi-pointes	
3		L on the whole foot, R pointe tendue à la seconde	L on the barre
4		close R in V devant	
1–4		V position, grand plié	R – bras bas – I – II
1–4		grand plié	R – III – I – II
1–2		demi-plié, 1 pirouette en dh	
3–4		pause (R retiré, L sur la demi-pointe)	
1–2		pause	
3–4		close R in V devant sur les demi-pointes	
1–4		bend sideways to the left	R – III
1–4		recover	R – II
1–7		3rd port de bras sur les demi-pointes	
8		demi-détourné into V L devant on the whole foot	R on the barre, L – II
1–4		V position, grand plié	L – bras bas – I – II
1–4		grand plié	L – III – I – II
1–2		demi-plié, 1 pirouette en dh	
3–4		pause (L retiré, R sur la demi-pointe)	
1–2		pause	
3–4		close L in V devant sur les demi-pointes	
1–4		bend sideways to the right	L – III
1–3		recover	L – II
4		demi-détourné into V R devant	L on the barre, R – II

Battement tendu

16	2/4	V R devant	R – bras bas
1			R – I – II
1–3	6 ♩	R 6 bts tendus devant, closing in demi-plié	
	♩	1 pirouette en dh,	
4	♩	finishing L on the whole foot with R pointe tendue à la seconde	R – II
1–3	6 ♩	R 6 bts tendus à la seconde, closing V derrière, devant . . . close V R devant in demi-plié	R – I
4	♩	1 pirouette en dh,	
	♩	finishing L on the whole foot with R pointe tendue derrière	R – II
1–8		repeat in reverse, close V R devant	

Battement jeté

16	2/4	V R devant	R – II
1–2	4 ♩	4 bts jetés en croix	
3	3 ♪	3 bts jetés devant	R – I – III
4	3 ♪	3 bts jetés à la seconde, closing V derrière, devant, derrière	R – I – II
1	3 ♪	3 bts jetés derrière	R – 2 arb
2	3 ♪	3 bts jetés à la seconde, closing V devant, derrière, devant	R – II
3	3 ♪	3 bts jetés à la seconde, each closing I	
4	3 ♪	3 bts jetés à la seconde, each closing I, and concluding V R derrière	
1–8		repeat in reverse	

Rond de jambe à terre

48	3/4	I position	R – bras bas
1–2		préparation en dh	R – I – II
1–2		2 ronds à terre	
3		3 ronds à terre,	
4		finishing R pointe tendue devant	
1–2		5 ronds à terre	
3–4		2 ronds à terre	
1		grand rond de jambe jeté	
2		rond à terre	
3		grand rond de jambe jeté	
4		rond à terre	
1–2		2 grands ronds de jambe jetés,	
3		finishing R pointe tendue devant	
4		pause	
1–16		repeat in reverse, finishing R pointe tendue derrière	
1–2		L deep fondu with R pointe tendue derrière	R – 2 arb
3–4		bend backwards	

1–2		transfer weight on R, L pointe tendue devant recover	R – I
3–4		bend backwards	R – III
1–2		recover	
3–4		L dégagé 90° devant sur la demi-pointe	
1		fouetté, finishing 2nd arb	R on the barre, L – 2 arb
2		pause	
3–4		close L in V devant on the whole foot	L – bras bas

Battement fondu

16	3/4	V R devant	R – bras bas
1–2		pause	
1–2		R bt fondu devant	R – I – II
3		R tombé en avant, finishing L dégagé 45° derrière	
4		1/2 tour en dh with L derrière 45°	
		R holding sur la demi-pointe, 1/2 pirouette en dh, finishing L devant 45°	L on the barre, R – I – II
1–2		R bt fondu derrière	R – bras bas – I – II
3		R tombé en arrière, finishing L dégagé 45° devant	
4		1/2 tour en dd with L devant 45°	
		R holding sur la demi-pointe, 1/2 pirouette en dd, finishing R derrière 45°	L on the barre, R – I – II
1–2		R bt fondu à la seconde 90°	R – bras bas – I – II
3		turning to the right (1/8) L fondu with R effacé devant	R – III
4		turning to the left (1/8) en face, L relevé with R à la seconde	R – I – II
1		turning to the left (1/8) L fondu with R effacé derrière	R – 2 arb
2		turning to the right (1/8) en face, L relevé with R à la seconde	R – II
3–4		L fondu, 2 pirouettes en dh, finishing R à la seconde 90°	
	♩	lower R à la seconde 45°	

Battement frappé

16	2/4		
1–2	6 ♪	R 6 bts frappés effacé devant, finishing en fondu	R – I – III
	♩	R cabriole fermée, finishing V R devant	
	♩	relevé in V	
3–4	6 ♪	L 6 bts frappés effacé derrière, finishing en fondu	
	♩	L cabriole fermée, finishing V L derrière	R – 1 arb
	♪	relevé in V	
1–2	6 ♪	R 6 bts frappés écarté derrière	R – III
	♪	close R in V derrière sur les demi-pointes	R – II
	♩	détourné into V R devant en face	
3–4		L fondu with R sur le cou-de-pied devant	R – I
		from temps relevé 2 pirouettes en dh, finishing R à la seconde 45° sur la demi-pointe	R – II
1–8		repeat in reverse	

Rond de jambe en l'air

16	2/4	V R devant	R – bras bas
1		préparation – temps relevé en dh	R – I – II
1	2 ♩	2 ronds en l'air en dh	
2	3 ♪	3 ronds en l'air en dh	
3–4	5 ♪	5 ronds en l'air en dh, finishing pointe tendue effacé devant en L fondu	R – I
	3 ♪	turning to the left (1/8) en face, L relevé with R à la seconde 45°	R – II
1	2 ♩	2 ronds en l'air en dh	
2	3 ♪	3 ronds en l'air en dh	
3–4	4 ♪	4 ronds en l'air en dh, finishing en fondu	
	♩	tour fouetté en dh, finishing R à la seconde 45° sur la demi-pointe	
	♩	double rond en l'air en dh	
1–8		repeat in reverse	

Adagio

24	3/4	V R devant	R – bras bas
1–2		pause	
1–2		R développé à la seconde sur la demi-pointe	R – I – II
3		flic-flac en tournant en dh, finishing R attitude devant	R – III
4		pause	
1–2	♩	L fondu tour en dh on L with R attitude devant	
3		R extended	R – III allongé
4		R tombé en avant, finishing L dégagé 90° derrière	
1		L piqué en arrière with R dégagé 90° devant	
2		close R in V devant sur les demi-pointes	R – II
3–4		3rd port de bras	
1–2			
3–4		R développé à la seconde	R – bras bas – I – II
1–2		demi-rond de jambe en dh, finishing attitude derrière	R – III
3		pause	
4		R tombé en arrière, finishing L pointe tendue devant	
1–2		bend backwards	
3		L piqué en avant into attitude derrière	R – I – III
4		1/2 tour en dd, finishing 4th arb	R on the barre, L – 4 arb

Battement double frappé

16	2/4	V R devant	R – bras bas
1	♩	relevé in V	R – I
	♩	R dégagé 45° à la seconde	R – II
1–2	4 ♩	4 bts doubles frappés en croix sur la demi-pointe	

3	♩	close R in V derrière in demi-plié	
	♩	détourné, finishing R pointe tendue effacé devant on L fondu	R – I
4		R bt battu effacé devant sur la demi-pointe, finishing turning to the left (1/8) en face, R à la seconde 45°	R – II
1–2		R petit bt sur le cou-de-pied (derrière–devant)	R – I – II
3	♪	L fondu with R sur le cou-de-pied devant	R – I
	♩	from temps relevé 2 pirouettes en dh, finishing R à la seconde 45° sur la demi-pointe	R – II
	♪	L fondu	
4	♪	R jeté dessus	R – I
	♪	emboîté on L with R sur le cou-de-pied devant	
	♩	L relevé with R petit développé à la seconde	R – II
1–8		repeat in reverse	

Grand battement

16	2/4	V R devant	R – bras bas
1–2			
1		R step en avant	R – I
		L cabriole devant	R – III
2	2 ♩	L 2 grands bts devant with R	
3	3 ♪	L 3 grands bts devant	
4		L bt développé devant sur la demi-pointe, finishing on the whole foot	
1		L step en avant	R – I
		R cabriole derrière	R – 2 arb
2	2 ♩	R 2 grands bts derrière with L	
3	3 ♪	R 3 grands bts derrière	
4		R bt développé derrière sur la demi-pointe, finishing on the whole foot	
1	2 ♩	R 2 grands bts à la seconde, closing V devant, derrière	R – II
2	3 ♪	3 grands bts à la seconde, closing V devant, derrière, devant	
3	3 ♪	3 grands bts à la seconde, closing V derrière, devant, derrière	
4		R bt développé à la seconde sur la demi-pointe, finishing V R devant on the whole foot	R – bras bas
1		R piqué en avant	R – I
		L through I into grand fouetté (to the right), finishing L derrière 90° en fondu	R on the barre, L – III allongé
2		L through I into grand fouetté (to the right), finishing L derrière 90° en fondu	L on the barre, R – III allongé
3		L through I into grand fouetté (to the right), finishing L derrière 90° en fondu	R on the barre, L – III allongé
4		pas de bourrée en dh into V L devant	L – II – bras bas

The Exercises in the Centre

Petit adagio

16	3/4	V L croisé devant	arms – bras bas
1–2		pause	
1		R piqué de côté to point 3, turning to the left (1/4) finishing facing 8, L attitude effacé devant 45° en fondu	arms – demi II allongé R – I, L – II
2	2 ♩	grand fouetté en effacé, finishing en R fondu	R – III – II, L – III
	♩	1 pirouette en dh on R,	
3		finishing facing 8, L attitude effacé devant 45° en R fondu	R – I, L – II
4		grand fouetté effacé, finishing en R fondu with L effacé derrière	R – III – II, L – III
1–2		pas de bourrée en dh into IV L croisé devant (préparation for pirouettes en dh)	arms – I – 1 arb
3		2 pirouettes en dh, finishing R attitude croisé derrière	R – III, L – II
4		pause	
1–2		renversé en dh, finishing IV R croisé devant (préparation for pirouettes en dd)	R – I, L – II
3–4		2 pirouettes en dd, finishing L attitude croisé devant	R – III, L – II
1–2		renversé en dd, finishing V R croisé devant	
3		R dégagé à terre croisé devant	arms – I to R – I, L – II
4		pause	

Battement tendu

8	2/4	IV R pointe tendue croisé devant	R – I, L – II
1		pause	
1		2 pirouettes-piqués en dd on R to point 2, finishing 1st arb à terre to point 2 on R	arms – I – 1 arb
2	2 ♩	L 2 bts tendus effacé derrière	
3		posé 2 pirouettes-piqués en dh on L, finishing R pointe tendue effacé devant	arms – II – I L – III, R – II
4	2 ♩	R 2 bts tendus effacé devant	
1	3 ♪	facing 2, L 3 bts jetés écarté devant, closing V devant, derrière, devant	L – I, R – II
2	3 ♪	R 3 bts jetés écarté derrière, closing V devant, derrière, devant	R – I, L – II
3–4	4 ♩	en face 4 bts tendus à la seconde (L, R, L, R), closing V devant	arms – I – II

Battement fondu

16	3/4	V R croisé devant	arms – bras bas
1–2		pause	
1–2		en face R bt fondu à la seconde 90° R tombé de côté, L coupé dessous	arms – I to R – III, L – II arms – II
3		grand jeté de côté on R with L sur le cou-de-pied devant finishing facing 2 (jeté porté)	arms – II allongé arms – bras bas
4		L bt fondu croisé devant 45°	arms – I to R – I, L – II

1–4		repeat with other foot	
1–2		en face R bt fondu à la seconde 90°	arms – I to R – III, L – II
		R tombé de côté, L coupé dessous	arms – II
3		grand jeté de côté, finishing facing 8 on R	arms – II allongé
		with L développé croisé derrière	arms – I – 3 arb
4	2 ♩	pause	
	♩	R relevé	
1–2		4 petits temps sautés en tournant en dh (to the left) in 3rd arb, finishing facing 8	
3		2 pirouettes en dh into V L croisé derrière in demi-plié	arms – I – II
4		détourné into V L croisé devant	arms – I – III

Petits temps sautés en tournant en dehors.

Pirouettes

8	2/4	V R croisé devant	arms – bras bas
1	♩	en face L relevé with R sur le cou-de-pied devant	arms – I
	♩	close R in IV croisé derrière (préparation for pirouettes en dh)	arms – 3 arb

1		2 pirouettes en dh into IV R croisé derrière	arms – I to L – I, R – II
2		2 pirouettes en dd into IV R croisé devant	arms – I – 3 arb
3		2 pirouettes en dh into IV L croisé derrière	arms – I to R – I, L – II
4	♩	2 pirouettes en dd into V L croisé devant in demi-plié	arms – I – bras bas
	♩	relevé	L – I, R – II

1		4 chaînés to point 7, finishing V R devant in demi-plié, en face	
	♪	relevé	R – I, L – II
2		4 chaînés to point 3, finishing V L devant in demi-plié, en face	
	♪	relevé	L – I, R – II
3		5 chaînés to point 7, finishing V R devant in demi-plié, en face	
	♪	relevé	R – I, L – II
4		5 chaînés to point 3, finishing 2nd arb à terre on R	

Grand adagio

34	3/4	V R croisé devant	arms – bras bas

1	R step en avant to point 2 into 2nd arb à terre	
2	pause	

1	facing 2, L piqué en arrière to point 6 with R dégagé 90° effacé devant	L – III, R – II
2	L fondu	
3–4	1 pirouette en dh, finishing facing 2, R effacé devant 90° on L fondu with bend backwards	arms – I to L – III, R – II

1	recover, R piqué en avant to point 2 into 1st arb	arms – I – 1 arb
2	R fondu	
3–4	1 pirouette en dd on R (sur le cou-de-pied derrière), finishing facing 2, 1st arb en R fondu with penché in arb	

1	recover, L piqué en arrière to point 6 with R dégagé 90° effacé devant, finishing L fondu	L – III, R – II
2	fouetté relevé (to the left), finishing 1st arb to point 6 en L fondu	arms – 1 arb
3	facing 6, close R in V devant sur les demi-pointes L développé derrière en R fondu	arms – bras bas arms – I – 1 arb
4	L through I into grand fouetté relevé (to the right), finishing 1st arb to point 2 en R fondu	arms – III – 1 arb

1–2	pas de bourrée en dh into wide IV L croisé devant (préparation for tours en dh)	arms – I – 3 arb
3–4	2 tours en dh on L in R attitude derrière, finishing facing 2	R – III, L – II
♩	L fondu	

1	1 pirouette en dh on L, finishing facing 8, R croisé devant 90° sur la demi-pointe	arms – III to R – III, L – II
2	R chassé en avant to point 8	arms – II
3	R tombé en avant into wide IV (préparation for tours en dd)	R – I, L – II
4	pause	

1	tour en dd on R in 1st arb, finishing facing 2 en fondu	arms – 1 arb
2	repeat tour	

3–4		2 pirouettes en dd on R, finishing 1st arb to point 2 en fondu	arms – I – 1 arb
1–3		pas de bourrée en dh into V L croisé devant en face R glissade de côté, finishing V L devant grand jeté de côté, finishing facing 8, on R with L développé croisé derrière close L in wide IV derrière (préparation for tours en dd)	arms – bras bas arms – II – I arms – II allongé arms – I – 3 arb R – I, L – II
4		pause	
1–2		2 tours en dd on R with L devant 90°, finishing facing 2, en fondu	R – III, L – II
3–4		1 pirouette en dd, finishing facing 2, en R fondu with L effacé derrière	arms – III to R – III, L – I arms – allongé

Grand battement

32	3/4 (mazurka)	V L croisé devant	arms – bras bas
1–2		pause	
1 2 3–4		turning to the left (1/4) facing 8, grande sissonne ouverte into attitude croisé derrière on R with bend backwards pas de bourrée en tournant en dh into V L croisé devant repeat 1–2 bars	arms – I to R – III, L – II arms – I – bras bas
1 2 3–4		facing 2, R grand bt effacé devant, closing IV devant L grand bt croisé devant, closing IV devant repeat 2 grands bts (R, L)	arms – I to R – III, L – II L – III, R – II
1 2 3–4		R grand bt in 3rd arb, closing IV croisé derrière L grand bt in 1st arb, closing IV effacé derrière repeat 2 grands bts in 3rd and 1st arb, finishing V L croisé devant	arms – I – 3 arb arms – 1 arb arms – bras bas
1–2 3–4		en face L 2 grands bts à la seconde, closing V derrière, devant R 2 grands bts à la seconde, closing V derrière, devant	arms – I – II
1–16		repeat the whole exercise in reverse	

Allegro

The First Exercise

8	2/4		V R croisé devant	arms – bras bas
1			facing 2, R sissonne tombé effacé en avant L coupé dessous R assemblé battu dessous	arms – I to R – I, L – II arms – II – bras bas
2 		♩ ♩	entrechat-quatre straighten knees	
3–4			repeat 1–2 bars with other foot, finishing V R croisé devant	
1	2	♩	2 assemblés battus dessus (L, R)	arms – bras bas
2 		♩ ♩	entrechat-quatre travelling en avant to point 8 straighten knees	arms – I to L – III, R – I arms – allongé

3	2 ♩	2 assemblés battus dessus (L, R)	arms – bras bas
4	♩	royale	arms – I – III
	♩	straighten knees	

The Second Exercise

8	2/4	V R croisé devant	arms – bras bas
1	♩	en face sissonne ouverte, finishing R petit développé à la seconde	arms – I – II
	♩	R double rond de jambe en l'air en dh sauté	
2	♩	grand jeté en avant to point 2 into 1st arb on R	arms – I – 1 arb
	♩	en face L glissade de côté, finishing V R devant	arms – I
3	♩	cabriole into 1st arb to point 2 on R	arms – 1 arb
	♪	L coupé dessous	
	♪	tour sissonne tombé to point 2,	
4		finishing R sissonne temps levé in 1st arb to point 2,	arms – I – 1 arb
		finishing V L croisé devant	arms – bras bas
1–4		repeat with other foot	

The Third Exercise

16	3/4	V R croisé devant	arms – bras bas
1–2		R sissonne tombé effacé en avant	arms – I to R – I, L – II
		turning to the left (1/4), facing 8, L coupé dessous temps levé in 2nd arb	arms – 2 arb
		facing 2, R chassé de côté to point 4	arms – II allongé
3–4		grand fouetté sauté en tournant,	arms – I – III
		finishing L attitude croisé derrière on R, facing 8	
1–4		repeat with other foot	
1		facing 2, R piqué en arrière to point 6 with L développé croisé devant	arms – I to R – II, L – III
2		R tombé en avant	arms – II
		R wide glissade en avant	arms – II allongé – I
3–4		grand pas de chat	R – III, L – I, arms – allongé
		R wide glissade en avant	arms – II allongé – I
1–4		repeat grand pas de chat	
		R sissonne tombé effacé en avant to point 2	arms – I – 1 arb
		cabriole in 1st arb on R	
		running to point 2	

The Fourth Exercise

16	3/4	IV L pointe tendue croisé devant en diagonale from point 6 to point 2	arms – demi II
1		pause	
2		R wide glissade en avant to point 2	arms – II allongé – I
1–2		pas de zephir into 1st arb on R	arms – III – 1 arb
3		R relevé in 1st arb	

4	♩	failli	arms – 4 arb
	2 ♩	R wide glissade en avant to point 2	arms – II allongé – I
1–2		pas de zephir into 1st arb on R	arms – III – 1 arb
3		R relevé in 1st arb	
4		facing 8, L chassé de côté to point 6	arms – II allongé
1–2		grand fouetté sauté en tournant, finishing 3rd arb on L to point 2 R coupé dessous	arms – I – III – 3 arb
3		facing 2, L piqué en avant into 3rd arb	arms – I – 3 arb
4		facing 4, R chassé de côté to point 6	arms – II allongé
1–2		grand fouetté sauté en tournant, finishing 1st arb on R to point 2	arms – I – III – 1 arb
3		facing 2, 3 temps glissés in 1st arb travelling en arrière to point 6	
4		R relevé in 1st arb	

The Fifth Exercise

16	3/4	IV L pointe tendue croisé devant en diagonale from point 6 to point 2	arms – demi II
1		pause	
2		R wide glissade en avant	arms – II allongé – I
1–2		grand jeté en avant in 2nd arb onto R L wide glissade en avant	arms – I – 2 arb arms – II allongé – I
3–4		into grand jeté en avant in 3rd arb onto L R wide glissade en avant	arms – I – 3 arb arms – II allongé – I
1–2		grand jeté en avant in 1st arb onto R	arms – I – 1 arb
3		R relevé in 1st arb	
4		facing 8, L chassé de côté to point 6	arms – II allongé
1–4		jeté entrelacé, finishing 1st arb on R to point 2 facing 8, L chassé de côté to point 6 jeté entrelacé, finishing 1st arb on R to point 2	arms – I – III – 1 arb arms – II allongé
1		R relevé in 1st arb	
2		failli into IV L croisé devant (préparation for pirouettes en dh)	arms – 3 arb
3		2 pirouettes en dh into IV R croisé derrière	arms – demi II
4		pause	

The Sixth Exercise

16	3/4	IV R pointe tendue croisé devant en diagonale from point 6 to point 2	R – I, L – II
1–2		posé pirouette–piqué en dh on L, finishing R développé écarté devant R tombé en avant, pas de bourrée en avant	R – III, L – II arms – II – I
3–4		grand pas de chat,	R – III, L – I, arms – allongé
		finishing facing 2, L fondu with R sur le cou-de-pied derrière	L – III, R – II
1–2		pas de bourrée en tournant en dh, finishing facing 8, R fondu with L sur le cou-de-pied derrière	arms – I R – III, L – II

3		L piqué en arrière to point 4 with R développé croisé devant	arms – I to L – III, R – II
4		R tombé en avant	arms – II
1–2		pas de bourrée en avant	
		grand jeté en avant in attitude croisé derrière onto R	arms – I to L – III, R – II
3		L step en avant	
		grand jeté en avant in attitude croisé derrière onto R	arms – I – II
4		L step en avant	
		grand jeté en avant in attitude croisé derrière onto R	arms – I – II
1		L glissade sur les demi-pointes en avant to point 8,	arms – I to L – III, R – I
		finishing V R croisé devant	arms – allongé
2		pause	
3–4		facing 2, R sissonne tombé effacé en avant	R – I, L – II
		L coupé dessous	
		grand jeté en tournant in attitude effacé derrière onto R	arms – I to L – III, R – II
	♩	R relevé in attitude	

The Seventh Exercise

8	3/4	V R croisé devant	arms – bras bas
		en diagonale from point 6 to point 2	
1	♩	facing 2, petit pas de basque on R, finishing L petit développé	arms – I to R – I, L – II
		croisé devant	arms – allongé
	2 ♩	2 steps en avant to point 2 (L, R)	
2	♩	grand pas de basque on L, finishing R développé effacé devant	arms – I – III – II
	2 ♩	2 steps en avant to point 2 (R, L)	
3–4		repeat 1–2 bars	
1	♩	en face R pas de chat to point 2,	arms – I – III
		finishing L fondu with R sur le cou-de-pied derrière	
	♩	L relevé with R petit développé à la seconde	arms – demi II allongé
	♩	R tombé dessus with L sur le cou-de-pied derrière	R – I, L – II,
			arms – allongé
2–3		repeat pas de chat and petit développé with L and R	
4		facing 8, IV R croisé devant in demi-plié	
		transfer weight on L, R pointe tendue croisé devant	arms – I – demi II

The Exercises sur les Pointes

The First Exercise

8	2/4	V R croisé devant	arms – bras bas
1	2 ♩	facing 2, R 2 ballonnés relevés effacé devant	arms – I to L – I, R – II
2	♪	L relevé with R petit développé écarté derrière,	arms – I – demi II allongé
	♪	finishing V R croisé derrière in demi-plié	
	♩	détourné into V R croisé devant	arms – bras bas
3	3 ♪	en face 3 échappés into II, changing position,	arms – I – II – bras bas
		finishing V L croisé devant	
4		facing 2, R relevé with L développé croisé devant,	arms – I to R – III, L – II
		finishing V L croisé devant in demi-plié	arms – II – bras bas
1–4		repeat with other foot	

The Second Exercise

8	2/4	V R croisé devant	arms – bras bas
1–2	3 ♩	R ballonné relevé devant 90°, turning to the right to points 3, 5, 8, finishing facing 8	arms – I to L – III, R – II
	♩	L relevé with R développé effacé derrière, finishing en fondu	arms – I – 2 arb
3		pas de bourrée en dh into V R croisé devant	arms – I – bras bas
4	♩	facing 8, L relevé with R double rond de jambe en l'air en dh écarté devant 90°, finishing V R croisé derrière in demi-plié relevé in V	arms – I to R – III, L – II arms – bras bas
1–4		repeat with other foot	

The Third Exercise

16	3/4	IV L pointe tendue croisé devant	arms – I with wrists crossed allongé
1		L piqué en avant to point 2, turning to the left en face, R développé à la seconde, finishing demi-rond de jambe en dd, facing 8	arms – II – III allongé
2	2 ♩	R tombé dessus with L sur le cou-de-pied derrière	arms – I with wrists crossed allongé
	♩	L coupé dessous	
3	2 ♩	R piqué en avant to point 8 into 3rd arb	arms – I – 3 arb
	♩	L coupé dessous	
4	2 ♩	R piqué en avant to point 8 into attitude croisé derrière	arms – I to L – III, R – II
	♩	R fondu	arms – II
1–2		renversé en dh, finishing V L croisé devant in demi-plié	arms – bras bas
3		L glissé en avant to point 7, relevé into 1st arb, finishing en L fondu	arms – I – 1 arb
4		pas de bourrée en dh, finishing facing 8, L fondu with R petit développé croisé devant	arms – bras bas – I
1–8		repeat with other foot	

The Fourth Exercise

16	3/4	IV L pointe tendue croisé devant	arms – I wrist crossed allongé
1		en face L relevé with R double rond de jambe en l'air en dd, finishing à la seconde 90°	R – III, L – II, arms – allongé
2		R tombé dessus with L attitude derrière à terre	R – I, L – II, arms – allongé
3–4		repeat with other foot	
1–2		repeat 1–2 bars with R foot, finishing facing 8, R fondu with L sur le cou-de-pied derrière	R – I, L – II, arms – allongé
3		pas de bourrée en tournant into V L croisé devant	arms – bras bas
4		facing 8, L step de côté to point 6 with R pointe tendue croisé devant	R – I, L – II

1–3		3 times posé pirouette-piqué en dh on L to point 2, finishing R développé écarté devant	arms – I to R – III, L – II
	♩	R tombé en avant to point 2	
4		L soutenu en tournant en dd into V R croisé devant	arms – I – III
1–4		repeat 1–4 bars (post pirouette-piqué en dh)	

The Fifth Exercise

8	2/4	V R croisé devant	arms – bras bas
1	♩	en face, L relevé with R double rond de jambe en l'air en dh, finishing L fondu	arms – I – II
	♩	pas de bourrée en tournant en dh into V R devant en face	arms – bras bas
2	♩	R relevé with L double rond de jambe en l'air en dh, finishing R fondu	arms – I – II
	♩	pas de bourrée en tournant en dd, finishing en face, L fondu with R à la seconde 45°	arms – I – II
3		pas de bourrée en tournant dessous-dessus	
4		repeat pas de bourrée, finishing R à la seconde 45° with L fondu	arms – I – II
1	♩	tour fouetté en dh, finishing R tombé dessus with L à la seconde 45°	
	♩	tour fouetté en dd, finishing L fondu dessous with R à la seconde 45°	
2–4	4 ♩	repeat twice tours fouettés en dh – en dd	
	♩	tour fouetté en dh, finishing V R croisé derrière	
	♩	relevé in V	arms – I – III

The Sixth Exercise

16	2/4	V R croisé devant en diagonale from point 6 to point 2	arms – bras bas
1	2 ♩	facing 2, R 2 ballonnés relevés effacé devant	arms – I to L – I, R – II
2	♩	L relevé with R petit développé écarté derrière, finishing L fondu	arms – I – demi II allongé
	♩	1 pirouette en dh on L, finishing facing 2, L fondu with R sur le cou-de-pied devant	arms – I
3	♪	R piqué sur la pointe en fondu en avant to point 2 into 1st arb	arms – 1 arb
	3 ♪	3 temps levés sur la pointe on R travelling en avant to point 2	
4	♪	R holding sur la pointe, straighten knee	
	♩	pause	
	♪	L coupé dessous	
1–4		repeat exercise, finishing relevé in V L croisé devant	
1–8		repeat with other foot	

The Seventh Exercise

8	2/4	IV R pointe tendue croisé devant en diagonale from point 6 to point 2	R – I, L – II
1–2	3 ♩	3 times pirouette-piqué en dd on R	
	♩	2 pirouettes-piqués en dd on R	
3–4	3 ♩	3 times posé pirouette-piqué en dh on L	
	♩	posé 2 pirouettes-piqués en dh on L	
1–4		repeat exercise, finishing IV R croisé derrière	arms – 3 arb

The Eighth Exercise

12	2/4	IV L devant in face (préparation for pirouettes en dh)	arms – 3 arb
1–12	24 ♩	24 tours fouettés, finishing IV R croisé derrière	arms – II

The Ninth Exercise

16	2/4	IV R pointe tendue croisé devant in a circle from point 8	R – I, L – II
1–16	32 ♩	32 pirouettes-piqués en dd on R, finishing 2nd arb on R to point 2	